WALK

# ILKLEY MOOR

# HILLSIDE GUIDES - ACROSS THE NORTH

WALKING COUNTRY

# ILKLEY MOOR

## Paul Hannon

**HILLSIDE**

# HILLSIDE
PUBLICATIONS
20 Wheathead Crescent
Keighley
West Yorkshire
BD22 6LX

First published 1994
Fully revised 2006
4th impression 2010

ISBN 1-978-870141-22-2

*Cover illustration: White Wells, Ilkley Moor*
*Back cover: Middleton Woods;*
*Doubler Stones; Leeds-Liverpool Canal, Farnhill*

*Page 1: On Skipton Moor*
*Page 3: Clapper bridge, Little London*
*(Paul Hannon/Hillslides Picture Library)*

The maps are based on 1947 Ordnance Survey One-Inch maps

Printed in Great Britain by
Carnmor Print
95-97 London Road
Preston
Lancashire
PR1 4BA

# CONTENTS

**INTRODUCTION**.................................................. 6

**THE WALKS** *(mileage in brackets)*

| | | |
|---|---|---|
| 1 | Otley Chevin (4½) | 10 |
| 2 | Burley Moor (5½) | 14 |
| 3 | The Ebor Way (5) | 17 |
| 4 | Baildon Moor (7) | 22 |
| 5 | Shipley Glen (7 or 3½) | 26 |
| 6 | Rombalds Moor (8½) | 30 |
| 7 | Doubler Stones (6) | 34 |
| 8 | Farnhill Moor (4) | 38 |
| 9 | Skipton Moor (6) | 42 |
| 10 | Bolton Abbey (7½) | 45 |
| 11 | Rombalds Way (6) | 49 |
| 12 | Chelker Reservoir (5½) | 53 |
| 13 | Windgate Nick (7½) | 56 |
| 14 | Buck Stones (5½) | 60 |
| 15 | Dick Hudson's (8 or 4) | 63 |
| 16 | Denton & Middleton (6) | 66 |
| 17 | Beamsley Beacon (7½) | 70 |
| 18 | Middleton Moor (6) | 74 |
| 19 | Kex Gill Moor (5½) | 78 |
| 20 | Blubberhouses Moor (6½) | 82 |
| 21 | Swinsty & Fewston (6) | 86 |
| 22 | Lindley Wood (7½) | 90 |

**WALK LOG**.................................................94

**USEFUL ADDRESSES**.........................................95

**INDEX**..................................................96

## INTRODUCTION

Who has not heard of Ilkley Moor, that bracing tract of heather upland that stands for all that is best about Yorkshire, county of the broad acres? Fewer, however, have set foot in this famous countryside, where rolling moors fall to the rich valleys and stately parkland that surround the buzzing town of Ilkley. Ilkley is very much the heart of this region, where the River Wharfe flows from the Yorkshire Dales. The Wharfe and Washburn Valleys are a buffer zone between the Dales and the Vale of York, and are little subservient to their National Park neighbour. Indeed, the Washburn Valley is within the Nidderdale Area of Outstanding Natural Beauty, while no-one could deny Ilkley and its moorland a place amongst the finest of English landscapes.

Ilkley itself is a thriving town that blends a workaday existence with that of a tourist venue. The Wharfe flows serenely by wooded banks just a stone's throw from the parish church, which boasts some of the finest Anglo-Saxon crosses. Alongside are the remains of a Roman fort, while the adjacent Manor House serves as a museum of local interest. Shops, pubs and cafes line spacious streets decorated with great pride by a tapestry of floral colour. The riverbanks play host to wide green spaces and a variety of sporting interests, while the graceful arch of the Old Bridge sends the Dales Way on its 80-odd mile course through the Dales to the Lake District. Ilkley has something for everyone, an attractive country town that does not shun its links with the outside world.

Once in Ilkley, one's eyes are constantly drawn to the moor: from the bustling pavements the great moorland bulk thrusts itself into the scene - dauntingly so on a grey day. On Ilkley's many sunny days, however, and never more than in late summer, this brooding mass of heather and gritstone exerts a powerful influence, and one is almost literally drawn to its airy heights. While town and moor may be synonymous, any one of the stiff pulls to the moor edge lead one into another world.

*Cross and stocks, Baildon*

6

Higher still, easier gradients reveal an expanse far greater than envisaged, and one can be striding over the heath, caressed by a refreshing wind far from the car-borne tourists. Gritstone edges and crags occur all over the moor, the major outcrops being around the world-famous Cow and Calf Rocks. Historically more significant are the innumerable evidences of early man, the moor being liberally dotted with stone circles, burial cairns, and the cup and ring markings that decorate many a dark boulder. In reality, Ilkley Moor is but one part of the great sweep of Rombalds Moor, which it must share with a host of individually named moors. Rombalds' upland ridge stretches from Skipton to Guiseley, a high boundary between Wharfe and Aire. Attractive settlements such as Micklethwaite, Burley Woodhead and Draughton repose on its flanks, while the valley floors echo to the throb of communications and industry.

The summit of Rombalds Moor reaches 1319ft/402m above sea level, but its northern counterpart across the Wharfe manages to oust it as the highest point in the book. Here, Round Hill overlooks a lonelier reach of moorland, again subdivided into the tracts above each of the settlements. The little communities bear no relation to those south of Rombalds Moor, however, being entirely rural, with the quietly farmed lower slopes interspersed by parkland belonging to great houses of centuries past. Into the 21st century the houses remain, echoes of an age largely consigned to the history books.

Finally the Washburn Valley, which again starts out on high moors, is another contrasting area, for while the Washburn flows into the Wharfe on the edge of busy Otley, its winding miles are in stark contrast. Here water rules the landscape, a chain of reservoirs harnessing the river in a manner that has largely blended well into the scene: now viewed as an integral feature, they are cushioned by wooded slopes that make their own contribution.

*On Otley Chevin*

## Getting around

Public transport to and within the area is good, with Ilkley's cul-de-sac railway station being the focal point. Lines from Leeds and Bradford serve both Wharfedale as far as Ilkley and Airedale as far as Skipton. Bus transport is equally good, with Skipton-Ilkley-Leeds, Keighley-Ilkley and Leeds/Bradford-Keighley-Skipton services supported by shorter runs serving villages in between. The Washburn area north of the Wharfe is less advantaged. While 4 of the 22 walks are described as linear rambles, any number of permutations can be created by linking different sections.

## Using the guide

Each walk is self-contained, with essential information followed by a simple map and concise description of the route. Dovetailed between this are useful notes of features along the way, and interspersed are illustrations which both capture the flavour of the walks and record the many items of interest. In order to make the instructions easier to follow, essential route description has been highlighted in bold type, while items in lighter type refer to historical asides and things worth looking out for: in this format you can find your way more easily while still locating features of interest at the relevant point in the text.

The simple sketch maps identify the location of the routes rather than the fine detail, and whilst the route description should be sufficient to guide you around, an Ordnance Survey map is recommended: the routes can easily be plotted on the relevant map. All but two walks (which overlap onto sheet 103) are found, conveniently, on Landranger sheet 104, Leeds, Bradford & Harrogate. To gain the most from a walk the detail of 1:25,000 scale maps cannot be matched: they also serve to vary walks as desired, giving an improved picture of one's surroundings and the availability of linking paths. The following sheets cover the walks as listed, with the first named being the principal companion to this guidebook, giving complete coverage of 16 of the 22 walks:

- **Explorer 297 - Lower Wharfedale & Washburn Valley:** 1-7,11-22
- **Explorer OL21 - South Pennines:** 8,9
- **Explorer 288 - Bradford:** 4,5
- **Explorer OL2 - Yorkshire Dales South/West:** 10,11

# WALKING COUNTRY - ILKLEY MOOR

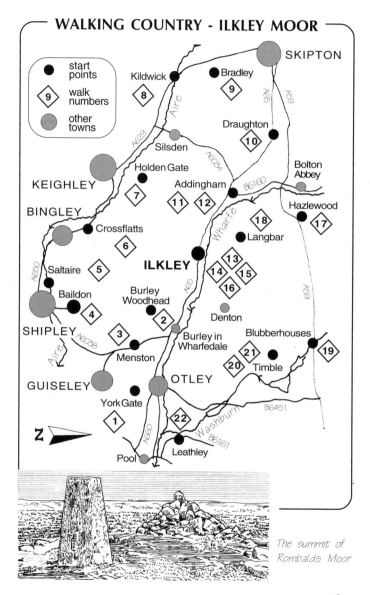

- **start points** (●)
- **◇9** walk numbers
- **●** other towns

SKIPTON

Kildwick
Bradley
◇8
◇9

Aire

Draughton
◇10

A629
A65
A59

Silsden
Holden Gate
Bolton Abbey

KEIGHLEY
Addingham
◇7
◇11  ◇12

BINGLEY
Hazlewood
◇18  ◇17

Crossflatts
◇6
Langbar

Wharfe
B6160

ILKLEY
◇13
◇14  ◇15
◇16

A660
Saltaire ◇5

Baildon
Burley Woodhead
Denton
Blubberhouses

◇4
◇2
◇19

SHIPLEY
◇3
Burley in Wharfedale
◇21
A59

B6038
Menston
◇20
Timble

Aire
OTLEY
B6451

GUISELEY
York Gate

Z
◇1
◇22
Washburn

Pool
Leathley
B6161
A660

The summit of
Rombalds Moor

9

# OTLEY CHEVIN

**START** York Gate        Grid ref. SE 204440

**DISTANCE** 4½ miles (7km)

**ORDNANCE SURVEY MAPS**
1:50,000
Landranger 104 - Leeds, Bradford & Harrogate
1:25,000
Explorer 297 - Lower Wharfedale & Washburn Valley

**ACCESS** Start at Beacon House car park on York Gate, west of the Royalty pub. An information board is provided by the City of Leeds, which runs the estate as the Chevin Forest Park. The midway point of Caley Crags makes a useful alternative start, being served by Otley-Leeds buses on the adjacent A660.

**❺ Go through the stile to emerge onto Surprise View on the crest of the Chevin.** The name, incidentally, is derived from the celtic 'cefn', meaning ridge or back. First feature of this expansive scene is the bird's-eye view of Otley itself. The countless other features are best saved for the end of the walk, when they will be better identified from the rocks up to the left. Having experienced a view as sweeping as anything to come, either return to the car, or commence the walk.

**A broad path runs along to the right on the top of Beacon Hill Moor, ignoring branches before ultimately dropping to join Miller Lane. Head along this gently declining track with its broad verge of brambles and bracken, gorse and heather, to reach East Chevin Road. A stile opposite leads into the woods of Danefield: this rises right, parallel with the road to reach Shawfield car park. Just yards to your left is a major fork.** A lime tree here was presented by Her Majesty the Queen in 1980 to commemorate the bi-centenary of the birth of Thomas Chippendale, Otley's famous cabinet-maker son.

Bear right on the main track - Chippendale Ride - into the plantations, and rising to a junction beyond a tiny beck, bear right again. This broad track climbs steeply away to trace the upper limit of plantings past an Ordnance column at 794ft/242m. Over to the right is the paraphernalia of Leeds-Bradford Airport at Yeadon.

Continue to a major junction at a corner, with trails radiating in all directions. Bear left off the main track on a broad break carrying tall pylons. Joining a track at the bottom, go left a short way to another junction. As the track swings left, pass through a kissing-gate in front and immediately fork right. This broad path curves down through open country to the crest of the lower grouping of Caley Crags. This is a fine place to linger, with opportunities for scrambling on a playground of boulders that offer serious rock climbing. The Wharfedale view returns almost to its earlier glory, with Otley along to the left. Down below is Pool, with its busy bridge over the Wharfe prominent, as is Almscliff Crag across the valley.

Resume left on the crest, with silver birch in bracken on the right. In deeper trees a kissing-gate puts you onto a broader track, keep straight on. At a major fork either option can be enjoyed: the lower track runs on beneath the major crags of Caley, affording good pictures from the jumbled boulders that have fallen off, while the upper track retains panoramic views before adding dramatic ones from the crest of the crags.

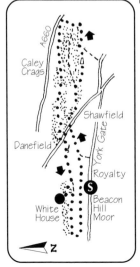

The upper path runs to a junction just before a footbridge. Don't cross it but turn steeply down a narrow path on the right thirty yards earlier to pick up the lower track at a crossroads. Re-united, go left to cross a stone bridge over the gill, passing an estate hut to travel a broad carriageway. This runs through the glorious surrounds of Danefield nature reserve to emerge back onto East Chevin Road at Danefield Gate. All the land on this side of the road was the Danefield estate and Caley Deer Park of Farnley Hall, presented to the town in 1946 by Major Horton-Fawkes as a memorial to their war dead.

Turn up the footway for 100 yards and cross to East Chevin Quarry car park. A broad path climbs away to run beneath quarried cliffs, easing out before moorland slopes are revealed below. These form a colourful foreground to Otley on the valley floor. **Further, woodland is re-entered and the path meets a broad track descending from the foot of Beacon Hill Moor.** Turn uphill for a direct return, if not visiting the White House. **For the full route bear right down the track, deeper into woodland to reach a crossroads with a steeply descending path. Just 100 yards further is the White House.**

Secluded in the trees, the White House is a former farmhouse turned visitor centre, with refreshments and toilets. It has long been a haunt of visitors and picnickers, though one must go round the front to appreciate its name.

*Ordnance Survey column, Danefield*

**Retrace steps to the crossroads where a flight of more than 200 steps make a very direct ascent to the foot of Beacon Hill Moor. Staggering onto the foot of the moor, if enough is enough go straight up to the waiting rocks on the Beacon site to be finished in two minutes. For further pleasures turn right on a broad path along the top of White House Plantation. It is shadowed by a fascinating vaccary wall of particularly thick slabs. These abruptly end but the path and trees remain. Some seventy yards beyond a broad path junction turn up a thin path immediately after an old wall. This rises through dense bilberry bushes to quickly join a higher level path, and doubling back along it past the Chevin's anonymous highest point the rocks are quickly gained.**

Now enjoy a final panorama from this eminent vantage point, identification of features aided by the presence of a rangefinder just below, on the Beacon House site. With distances in miles, it picks out man-made creations such as the masts on Emley Moor 20 and Holme Moss 26, York Minster 26, Arthington Viaduct 4, Kilburn White Horse 30, and Ferrybridge Power Station 21. Distant natural features include Great Whernside high in the Yorkshire Dales; and Boulsworth

Hill on the Lancashire border. Nearer to hand, across the Wharfe, are more regular contributions from this area, including Farnley Hall, Denton and Middleton Moors, and Beamsley Beacon.

The Beacon House, known as Jenny's Cottage after one of its former occupants, was finally fully demolished in 1976. This has been the setting for many a bonfire, to warn of approaching danger or more usually to celebrate happy, invariably royal, events. It is also the location of a great wooden cross, around 30ft in height, erected annually to mark the start of Holy Week leading up to the feast of Easter. Its siting is clearly visible to townsfolk in the streets below.

*Caley Crags, looking across the valley to Almscliff Crag*

# BURLEY MOOR

**START** *Burley Woodhead*        *Grid ref. SE 148453*

**DISTANCE** *5½ miles (9km)*

**ORDNANCE SURVEY MAPS**
*1:50,000*
*Landranger 104 - Leeds, Bradford & Harrogate*
*1:25,000*
*Explorer 297 - Lower Wharfedale & Washburn Valley*

**ACCESS** *Start from a lay-by between two sharp bends at the foot of Burley Moor, on the Ilkley side of Burley Woodhead. A short open section of road above Moor Lane offers further room at the foot of the moor, while a walk up Moor Lane from Burley station also brings arrival here.*

**§** **Go through the gate and straight up the path climbing steeply above Coldstone Beck.** Extensive views look over Burley, back to Otley Chevin and to the vast moors across the valley. Immediately below is Moor House, a former youth hostel. **When the path climbs further from the beck, fork left to contour in towards it, meeting a broader path to drop down to cross the stony gill. After a clamber up**

*Horncliffe circle*

the opposite bank, the path runs level. Ignore an early branch left, and within a minute double back right at a major path crossroads. The path rises to a plateau, over another cross-paths and gently up again, parallel with Coldstone Beck over to the right. On a modest edge the path swings right, rising through heather to suddenly reach Lower Lanshaw Dam. From here the path bears right through an old retaining wall and makes for the Grubstones on the near skyline.

**Just before the stones the path crosses a broad track, and easily missed yet simply located is Grubstones stone circle. Going left on the track to a wooden cabin, the circle lurks just 60 yards behind in the heather.** Some 20 stones of this burial cairn survive within a 10 yards diameter. **Back at the outcrops note the appearance of High Lanshaw Dam: this fine viewpoint is a great spot to linger. Leave by locating a thin path heading off through the heather from the easternmost of the stones. It becomes clearer and gradually nears a fence as it moves to the farthest corner of Burley Moor.**

Forty yards over the fence on Hawksworth Moor, after a boundary stone (inscribed *Hawksworth/Pulleyn* - see overleaf) and just before crossing Horncliffe Beck, stands Horncliffe stone circle (GR 134435). Another burial cairn, it is just 8 yards in diameter and contains around 50 stones side by side, also enclosing a smaller, hollowed circle.

*The Horncliffe Stone,*
*Hawksworth Moor*

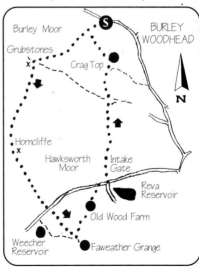

15

Approaching a wall, the site of Horncliffe House is reached, just before the corner. Over the fence all that remains is the base: a wall-stile permits investigation. Adjacent is a stone inscribed *WH Horncliff Well*, and at the stile another 'well' stone bears the names *Thomas Pulleyn* and *Sr Walter Hawksworth*: a clear spring emerges into a stone trough. Back over the stile a largely good path drops through an intervening wall-stile to a busy moor-edge road, with Weecher Reservoir ahead. Cross straight over and down three fieldsides to a grassy bridge on a stream, then up a short enclosed way to emerge via a yard onto a walled lane at Little London. The junction of ways just past here has existed since monastic times, and continued to see much activity in packhorse days - hence the name given to it by travellers. Both your approach to and return from Little London are on ancient routes linking Baildon and Ilkley.

Advance just a few yards and double back left down a walled way to a ford and clapper bridge on Gill Beck (illustrated on page 3), then up the similar way of Old Wood Lane, with an old stone causey in evidence. It runs to Old Wood Farm, continuing out on its drive onto the moor-edge road just short of a junction at Intake Gate. This is also known as the Gaping Goose, after a long-closed inn. From a gate to the left of the house follow a wallside path onto Hawksworth Moor. When the wall turns right stay with it, but after 130 yards strike left on a path slanting up to a gate in a fence. The brow behind reveals the setting of an old rifle range.

Contour right towards a green hut to follow a track up to the range top. Cross the access road and within yards a slim path heads off, winding round towards a telegraph pole. Cross a track climbing the moor (the shooters' track to Grubstones cabin) and drop down to a wallside rough road. Follow it left as far as a second farm (York View) where it leaves the moor. Remain on a moor-edge track to a big quarry alongside the austere house of Crag Top (1861 datestone), then a colourful track curves down steeper slopes to look down on the start of the walk, alongside a farm.

Either continue straight down, utilising a sunken way to the moor-foot by the old Chapel School above Moor Lane; or return directly to the starting gate by slanting left, a labyrinth of paths crossing the plateau above the distinct crest of Barks Crag to Coldstone Beck and those outward steps. Alternatively, take a lower path above the intake wall to Coldstone Beck nearer the starting gate.

# THE EBOR WAY

**( 3 )**

**START** Menston     *Grid ref. SE 174440*

**FINISH** Ilkley     **DISTANCE** *5 miles (8km)*

**ORDNANCE SURVEY MAPS**
*1:50,000*
*Landranger 104 - Leeds, Bradford & Harrogate*
*1:25,000*
*Explorer 297 - Lower Wharfedale & Washburn Valley*

**ACCESS** *Menston and Ilkley are 10 minutes apart on the Wharfedale railway line, which has a regular service. They are also linked by bus. Ample parking outside Menston station.*

The Ebor Way is a gentle 70 mile walk from Helmsley through York to Ilkley, linking the Cleveland Way with the Dales Way. This walk shadows its final miles into Ilkley, unquestionably its finest moment.

**S** **From the station entrance head straight up Cleasby Road, turning right along Main Street,** passing shops, pubs, and just to the right down Burley Lane, the parish church on a green knoll. The village of Menston has grown into an extensive commuterland serving the big cities of Leeds and Bradford. It was renowned for its imposing psychiatric hospital High Royds, which treated the ill for over half a century before closure at the end of the 20th century.

**Near the edge of the village, hidden on the right is Menston Old Hall.** Dated 1653, it is known as Fairfax Hall after its connections with that famous family. Sir Thomas Fairfax, an important ally of Oliver Cromwell, spent time here before the monumental encounter at Marston Moor in 1644. **A little beyond the hall, when the road swings left as Moor Lane, bear right on Bleach Mill Lane.** Before leaving the road note Grange Farm on the right, a lovely old house with mullioned windows and a 1672 datestone.

**17**

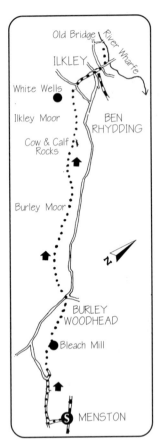

Old Bridge
River Wharfe
ILKLEY
White Wells
Ilkley Moor
BEN RHYDDING
Cow & Calf Rocks
Burley Moor
N
BURLEY WOODHEAD
Bleach Mill
S MENSTON

The rough road runs on between modern houses then as an improving byway with extensive Wharfedale views. Just before reaching Bleach Mill House an attractive mill pond is seen. Without entering its confines leave the drive by a snicket to the left. Beyond a stile is a path junction where a stream comes splashing down amidst much greenery. A track continues along the wallside to a stile to approach Hag Farm and its attendant jumble. A gate by the right-hand barn keeps you outside its yard, a wall then runs to another snicket onto a drive at Spring Bank's attractive gritstone houses. Cross to a kissing-gate in front and head across a couple of fields to emerge onto another drive. This time rise to the road at Burley Woodhead. While the route turns right, the *Hermit Inn* is just along to the left. Portrayed on the sign is 19th century character Job Senior. At the age of 60 he wed a lady 20 years his senior in order to acquire a nestegg when she passed on. He maintained his reputation for drinking money away, but on her demise her family claimed his legacy. In Job's absence their cottage was pulled down, but he built a hut on the spot and lived there in squalor. The hermit became an object of great interest, almost a tourist attraction. Falling ill at a local pub, he died aged 77.

*Cow & Calf Rocks*

*Hermit Inn, Burley Woodhead, in 1984 livery*

Turning right for 60 yards, the route takes to the moor at the head of Burley in Wharfedale's Moor Lane. A gate gives access to the foot of Burley Moor, adjacent to the old Chapel School, closed in the 1960s. Take the main path climbing alongside a sunken way. On easing when level with an old farm, bear right on an inviting branch along the defined edge of Barks Crag. Outstanding views over the valley now remain throughout. Below is distinctive Moor House, until the 1970s a youth hostel providing almost 100 beds.

Stay on the main path which runs on to approach Coldstone Beck, slanting down to cross it before a steeper pull up the opposite slope. The walk resumes along a distinct edge, initially with a wall for company. With the road never distant below, the path runs on through the colourful terrain of Green Crag Slack. Soon the *Cow & Calf Hotel* and then the rocks themselves appear, and the highly distinctive Pancake Stone is encountered. Its flat top is awash with cup marks, their exact purpose unknown but Bronze Age in origin.

Before this point you might stray beneath the edge, as a more obvious path takes you beneath the hanging rock of the Pancake Stone to cross to the Cow and Calf, while immediately below the

**Pancake a green quarry track runs down to Hangingstone Road, and another track crosses to the rocks. The higher path remains on the edge to reach another individual stone, the Haystack Rock.** Sat back from the edge, it is inscribed with further cup marks. **From here a descent is finally made to the waiting Cow and Calf Rocks.**

These esteemed outcrops constitute one of Yorkshire's premier landmarks, and their roadside location sees them regularly swarm with trippers. On a hot, sunny day the temptation of ice cream will delay the attractions of exploring the rocks, which until modern day romanticism were known as the Hanging Stones. This is a hugely popular climbing area, with substantial rockfaces easy of access. The main buttress of the Cow, however, is so bold and uncompromising that most climbers will be found in the great bowl of the quarry round the back, with the added advantage of a south-facing outlook to put the sun on their backs. Close by is the roadside *Cow & Calf Hotel.*

Looking down Wharfedale from Barks Crag

The great, sloping top of the Cow is remarkable for its array of carvings, not Bronze Age but largely 19th century immortality seekers. While some of these are incredible works, modern, sub-standard efforts have badly defaced this and various other rocks in the locality. Below the Cow is its offspring the Calf, whose scooped steps offer an easy angled scramble for the casual visitor, a near-obligatory challenge! Immediately below is the vast well-to-do sprawl of Ben Rhydding, which though basically a much enlarged suburb of Ilkley, is the former settlement of Wheatley, overtaken by the hydropathy craze of the 19th century. The first such establishment was built here in the 1830s, and the name Ben Rhydding has stuck firm ever since.

**From the quarry behind the Cow, a path runs on to enter a small plantation with a much larger quarry site to the left. Emerging back onto the moor, paths work steeply down to a footbridge over Backstone Beck, from where a level path quickly runs on to The Tarn. Here urban paths materialise, and at its far end one runs to the foot of the moor, where a road descends into the town.** Note, incidentally, that from the far end of The Tarn a detour up to White Wells is possible, passing a smaller tarn en route. More detail is found on the walk to *Dick Hudson's*.

**Part way down Wells Road, go left to enjoy a nicer descent through the gardens of Wells Promenade onto the main shopping thoroughfare, The Grove. The station is just along to the right, while the appropriate conclusion is straight down, crossing the main road by the church and descending to the riverbank. A path leads upstream to the Old Bridge, where the Dales Way eagerly absorbs the Ebor Way's final steps.**

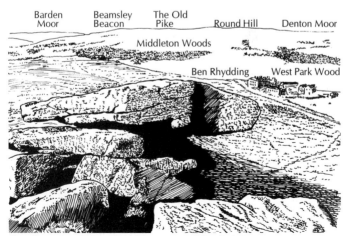

*The Pancake Stone, looking across Wharfedale*

# BAILDON MOOR

**START** *Baildon*          *Grid ref. SE 155397*

**DISTANCE** *7 miles (11km)*

**ORDNANCE SURVEY MAPS**
*1:50,000*
*Landranger 104 - Leeds, Bradford & Harrogate*
*1:25,000*
*Explorer 288 - Bradford & Huddersfield*
*Explorer 297 - Lower Wharfedale & Washburn Valley*

**ACCESS** *Start from the market cross in Towngate in the heart of the village. Car park and buses adjacent; rail station one mile.*

**S** Baildon was an important market site in centuries past: packways radiated in all directions, many over the moors to Ilkley, Addingham and beyond. The market cross is of medieval origin, with adjacent stocks. **From the roundabout turn up Hallcliffe past the Ian Clough Hall.** This recalls a Baildon climber tragically killed on Annapurna in 1970. **Pass the parish church to a once important junction: ahead is the old packway of Ladderbanks Lane, while your equally historic route is Heygate Lane up to the left. At the junction at the end keep on a clubhouse drive, and on again on a surfaced path between sports fields. Briefly enclosed, it runs on to a small gate onto a corner of Baildon Moor.** Ahead is the straggling line of Hawksworth.

**Just in front, the lane known as Moorside drops to an equestrian centre.** Miners' and quarrymens' cottages existed here until the 1960s. A seat offers a lovely prospect over the colourful valley you are about to cross to Hawksworth. **Just short of the buildings drop to a small gate and an enclosed path drops straight down alongside a paddock. Emerging at the bottom continue down the fieldsides, crossing to the other side at a stile to descend to a leafy glade and over a grassy brow into the sylvan charms of Hawksworth Spring.**

Cross the beck by stepping-stones, and opt for the path slanting right, climbing pleasantly through woodland to a wall-stile into a field. Continue rising, soon transferring to the other side by stile and slab footbridge to a corner of a golf course. The way rises unswervingly through a series of stiles, and a final pair lead across a yard to a narrow way between houses onto the road through Hawksworth. Hawksworth is a house-proud village clinging to a busy minor road. Looking as rural as Arncliffe or Linton, it sits just outside the suburban limits of Guiseley, which merges into the great city of Leeds. To the right are delightful gritstone cottages with manicured lawns and roses round the doors, while at the far end is the hall, currently a school.

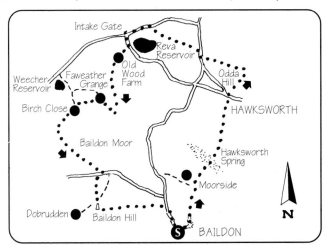

Opposite, a snicket winds up behind a house and rises by an attractive wood. A kissing-gate puts you onto Odda Hill, where a faint path advances to the brow of the field to be greeted by an extensive Wharfedale panorama. Keep on, however, to a colourful gorse bank, NOW rest awhile. Below is Menston; to the right is Guiseley, with the hinterland of the Chevin rising beyond Menston; Otley sits in the Chevin's shadow. Across the Wharfe the vast moors of Denton and Askwith sweep round the northern skyline.

Descending the bank, ignore a stile at the bottom and turn left on a grassy track which runs a largely splendid course to meet Hillings Lane opposite stables at East View. Go briefly right to a stile opposite, crossing the yard to a stile at the end. Follow the wall rising away to be ushered right to a pair of stiles onto the foot of a corner of open country. A smashing path rises away, passing left of the knoll ahead, with Reva Reservoir below. The access road to its sailing centre leads out to the busy Bingley Road. Ahead are the inviting Hawksworth moors. **Go left with caution, the initial brow being the only dodgy moment. A broad verge materialises for a two-minute walk to a junction at Intake Gate,** once an inn of dubious clientele known as the *Gaping Goose*. **Cross the side road then take an immediate stile on the left, to a path along a narrow way between wall and beck.** In this hidden corner an unexpected little ravine is lodged between heather verges.

**Approaching Intake Farm take a stile on the right and down to another in the bottom corner. Now strike across the field to locate a good stile into the environs of Old Wood Farm. Go left of a modern barn and on to a wall-stile ahead. Now simply head away with the wall, descending through intervening walls to the wooded environs of Gill Beck, hugely colourful terrain. At the bottom bear left through crumbling walls to find a path descending the wooded bank to cross the tiny beck. Up the other side a stile admits to a tiny walled snicket, then up a mini golf course to a stile. Bear left at the nearest of a group of wooden cabins below old quarries, their access track rising onto Sconce Lane by way of a stile right of the ornate gate. Double back right on this unmade way, enjoying immediate views over Old Wood and the preceding mile en route to Faweather Grange.** Originally this was a small grange of Rievaulx Abbey: the monks mined ironstone nearby, while a stone mine opened as recently as 1889 was worked to a depth of 90 feet for flags and roofing stone.

*Faweather Grange*

At a junction beyond the grange go left around the back of **Faweather Farm on another walled lane rising to an open tract. Keep on along the back of renovated Birch Close, and just past it enter Birch Close Lane.** Equestrian use has obliterated this ancient moorland packway from Shipley to Ilkley via Faweather and Gaping Goose. **A sandy track takes over and quickly merges with another: emerging into a field advance to a fork, keeping straight on down to a gate at a wall corner ahead to enter a corner of Baildon Moor.**

Baildon Moor is shared with many other leisure users, though prime concern is an awareness of golf balls. **After a few steps on the broad path fork left past a tee and alongside a fairway. Beyond the green bear left up a clear path slanting up Pennythorn Hill. With the open road close by, pass another green to join it at a parking area. Cross to ascend a grassy track, rising to a brow to reveal the moortop OS column, before which make for a curious tor-like feature beneath it.** The moor was mined for coal from at least 1387, and later for steam engines for mills: the last pit closed about a century ago. What we have here are slagheaps - locally the 'cinder caves'.

**Cross Dobrudden farm road to rise to the summit of the walk, the trig. point at 925ft/282m on Baildon Hill.** The panorama reaches to distant power stations beyond Bradford, and along the Pennine crest to Keighley. Bingley Moor represents the Rombalds Moor expanse.

Baildon Moor was purchased by Bradford Corporation for £7000 in 1897, and in the 1920s was the scene of illegal gambling rings. **Striking east a broad path (one of many) crosses the plateau to reveal Baildon village, with the church tower prominent. A track descends the bracken bank to the near wall corner, remaining on the moor twixt a fairway and housing, with much flagging underfoot. At the foot of the moor the golf clubhouse drive leads onto a road which joins Moorgate to descend into the village.**

*The path at Hawksworth Spring*

## 5

# SHIPLEY GLEN

**START** Saltaire          Grid ref. SE 139380

**DISTANCE** 7 miles (11km) (3½ miles/5½km one-way only)

**ORDNANCE SURVEY MAPS**
1:50,000
Landranger 104 - Leeds, Bradford & Harrogate
1:25,000
Explorer 288 - Bradford & Huddersfield
Explorer 297 - Lower Wharfedale & Washburn Valley

**ACCESS** Start from the railway station on the Airedale line.

Saltaire was created as a mill village by Sir Titus Salt, who moved his workers to this green-field site from the polluted air and slums of Bradford. From 1850 to 1872 hundreds of terraced stone dwellings were built to house the workforce of his new worsted processing mill. This outstanding piece of industrial architecture, 550ft long and 6 storeys high, is a sight to behold. The village's grid-iron system remains virtually intact, along with the schools, almshouses, hospital and institute that followed. Salt's notable omission was a public house. Most buildings function as originally intended, and this major conservation area was designated a World Heritage Site in 2001.

**⑤** **From the railway station turn down Victoria Road.** Note, in spacious grounds, the finest of Salt's buildings: the remarkable Congregational Church (now the United Reformed Church) was built in 1859 in rich Italian style, with a semicircular front and ornate circular tower. **The road crosses the Leeds-Liverpool Canal to the** *Boat House Inn* **on the River Aire, and a large metal pedestrian bridge gives access to Roberts Park.** A tribute to Salt's work, the park was an important amenity for his millworkers. **Head away from the bridge through the edge of the park onto Higher Coach Road, with a row of shops and the** *Cup & Ring* **pub to the right.**

Alternatively, cut through the park to see the fine statue of Salt erected in 1903 on the centenary of his birth, and pick up the route on Higher Coach Road. Bearing left along it, an urban path strikes across playing fields to the foot of the wooded bank, and the bottom station of the **Shipley Glen Tramway, 'Gateway to the Moors'.** The Shipley Glen Cable Tramway was built in 1895, and its open cars haul visitors up the wooded bank towards the attractions of the glen. Restored after a period in the doldrums, it survives today only precariously, hard-pushed by vandalism and modern insurance demands.

*Shipley Glen Tramway*

**To its left a surfaced path climbs by Trench Wood to the top station. Go left along suburban Prod Lane, passing the site of an old funfair and pleasure grounds. Just further along is the *Old Glen House* pub with adjacent tearooms. Directly behind is the open country of the glen itself. Strike out across the grassy terrain, the best line being along the crest of a broken gritstone edge that quickly forms above the wooded bank. This avoids the traffic though not all of the people, and serves the route well throughout the length of the glen.**

A brief diversion could take in the roadside Bracken Hall, operating as a countryside centre with exhibitions and displays on local history and wildlife. It also organises activities aimed largely at the young 'uns.

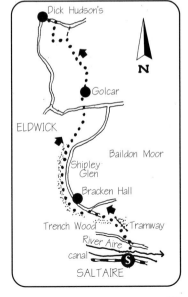

The glen has been a place of popular resort since people first escaped city grime for weekend fresh air. Known as Brackenhall Green until the romanticised 'glen' was appended in the 1840s, its proximity to the Bradford metropolis has always ensured a regular stream of visitors. The depths of the glen are rich in natural woodland, though most folk tend to perambulate along the spacious green. Only 100 yards past the hall is the Soldiers' Trench, a Bronze Age circle originally up to 50 yards across. Though part destroyed by the road, a double circle of at least 60 stones may still be seen.

**The path now runs above more substantial rocks, decorated in dry spells by the chalk of climbers.** Set back up to the right is Baildon Moor, site of Bronze Age earthworks. Today one can observe modern man doing his own thing, be it pony-trekking, biking, rambling, climbing, model aircraft, hang-gliding.... **Towards the end the road squeezes in again, and when the attendant wall turns up the moor, a parting of the ways is reached: the road bears right, while a broad pathway goes left to the upper confines of the glen. Your route is the grassy way directly ahead, traversing level ground above a big quarry site, now reclaimed by heather and**

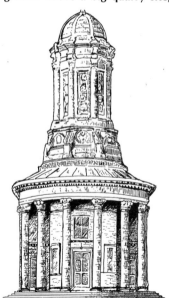

**popular with scrambling bikes. Broadening to cross a similar way, advance on the slimmer continuation towards the trees ahead. The path runs to the edge of the moor, a tiny footbridge leading to a small gate and a smashing path sets off to shadow tree-girt Glovershaw Beck.** Approaching a minor confluence a boundary stone inscribed *WTB* stands by the path. Here also was the site of a bloomery, operated under the auspices of the monks of Rievaulx Abbey, who mined ironstone on the moor from the grange at nearby Faweather.

*Saltaire United Reformed Church*

The path runs on below a paddock, deflected left of barns at Glovershaw and staying with the beck to emerge at a furtive stile onto Glovershaw Lane on the Eldwick-Baildon boundary. Fading paint on the farm proclaiming 'TEAS' recalls the days when refreshment might be found at any number of wayside farms. **Cross over and up the drive opposite to reach the attractive range of buildings at Golcar Farm.** Astride a crossroads of old ways, this approach is on the line of a monastic route linking a grange at Bingley with the smaller Faweather Grange. In addition, coming in from Baildon Moor is an old way that continues up towards the moor road near *Dick Hudson's:* this you shall follow, with a variation at the end.

**Don't turn into the yard but continue to a bridle-gate on the left at the end of the buildings. Advance straight on to the start of a green pathway rising steadily between fields, emerging to run left with a wall to the next stile. Maintain the line across a field, rising steadily to a wall-corner. From the gate rise with a wall again to a gate onto a drive which climbs towards Otley Road. Halfway up, however, at a kink, take a wall-stile on the left, and with *Dick Hudson's* now prominent up to the left, cross the field bottom and resume up the far wallside. When it turns off continue straight up towards Eldwick Crag Farm, emerging by a stile onto Otley Road.**

**Don't leap too enthusiastically onto it, it can be busy. *Dick Hudson's* is just two minutes to the left.** Please turn to WALK 15 for a note on *Dick Hudson's.* If you wish to continue this famous trek over Ilkley Moor to Ilkley itself, then that is the walk to consult from here. The alternatives are to have a friendly driver waiting at the bar; retrace steps; or descend Bingley Road to pick up a bus above Eldwick.

*Shipley Glen*

## 6

# ROMBALDS MOOR

**START** *Crossflatts*     *Grid ref.  SE 102405*

**DISTANCE** *8½ miles (13½ km)*

**ORDNANCE SURVEY MAPS**
*1:50,000*
*Landranger 104 - Leeds, Bradford & Harrogate*
*1:25,000*
*Explorer 297 - Lower Wharfedale & Washburn Valley*

**ACCESS** *Directions begin from the village centre, where Micklethwaite Lane strikes up past the Royal pub just up from the railway station. Numerous bus services operate along the old main road.*

**S** **Follow the lane up to the Leeds-Liverpool Canal at Micklethwaite Wharf and turn left on the towpath as far as the next swing bridge on Morton Lane.** Morton Lane, immediately below the swing bridge, is a good alternative car parking start (GR 099411).

**Cross the bridge and within yards take a gap-stile on the right. An enclosed path heads away, rising into trees then slanting more faintly up a field.** Fine views look to Micklethwaite across the side valley of Morton Beck. **At the top a wall leads along to a stile onto an urban road on the edge of East Morton. Advance a few yards to turn right at a T-junction. Again within yards, turn up a cobbled drive on the left from where a walled snicket rises to emerge via an attractive fold onto Otley Road. Cross with care and up a short flight of steps to head along Green End Road.** Dramatic views look through gaps between houses to a mill dam nestling below.

**Leaving the terraces behind, a fork is reached in front of the grounds of Morton Hall. Take the rough road left (Upwood Lane), and at a junction below a farm go right, a good track heading away to rise through colourful surrounds to enter wooded Sunnydale. As the track swings to cross the beck, advance to the dam of Sunnydale**

**Reservoir, a tranquil scene of woodland and water. Across, a path climbs the bank to a junction.** An alternative path runs left through Sunnydale to emerge onto the main route at Bradup Beck. **From the stile in front ascend the wallside to isolated Glen Farm, and from a stile at the top go right to join the drive alongside the entrance gate.**

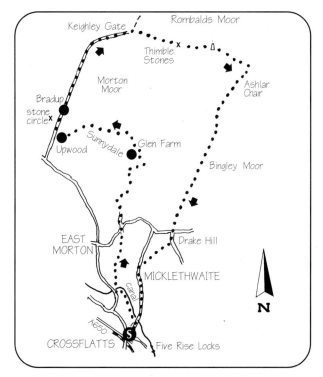

**Without entering the farm take a gate opposite, from where a grassy track winds up through the fields, passing a small, roofless barn with the moor edge just above. Crossing tiny Sweet Well Dike above a pocket wood, the track runs through more fields to enter woodland enshrouding Bradup Beck. Now firmer underfoot, it emerges on the other side to run on towards Upwood Hall, but avoid the adjacent farm by turning sharp right just before it to follow a wall up onto Ilkley Road.** Upwood was the home of the Busfeild family whose arms adorn the pub back in the village.

**Turn right along this old road to the moor.** Within yards, at a gate on the left, the old Bingley-Addingham trading route starts a direct march over the moors, but down to its right on the moor just past a small enclosure are the remains of Bradup stone circle. A dozen or so stones survive, less than half the original complement. The name Brass Castle on maps suggests that a Roman signal station may have been sited here alongside their road from Manchester to Ilkley. **Ilkley Road drops to cross Bradup Beck at lonely Bradup then climbs onto Rombalds Moor, passing a stone spring dated 1853. Useful verges lead along to the road summit at Keighley Gate (Whetstone Gate on maps)** a popular parking spot for Keighlians. **Through the gate leave the now unsurfaced road, and turn up a wallside path (some flagged sections) past the twin radio masts to gain the more endearing landmarks of the Thimble Stones.** Here one can survey the freshly revealed country of Wharfedale. Pride of the Thimble Stones are a brace of boulders amid a host of smaller rocks, the majority being found over the wall.

**The direct path remains with the wall for a short mile to Ashlar Chair, but more rewarding is a visit to the summit of Rombalds Moor. While a wet path runs across to the OS column, better to follow the wallside path until level with it, where a thin path runs out to the trig. point and cairn at 1319ft/402m.** The extensive view offers a host of features across the valley, from Buckden Pike and Great Whernside at the dalehead down to Simon's Seat, Beamsley Beacon, Round Hill, Lippersley Ridge, Menwith Hill, Almscliff Crag and Otley Chevin: westward are two proud Lancashire landmarks, Boulsworth Hill and Pendle Hill. **A better, broader path runs east from the summit, declining gently to a slight edge at White Crag Moss. The improved path runs on to pass above a colourful boulder cluster, a good spot to linger before losing the Wharfedale panorama. Just past here is a crossroads with a fainter path linking the Dick Hudson's path with Ashlar Chair. A right turn here leads back up to the brow, and the ridge-wall at Ashlar Chair.** This biggest boulder in the vicinity marks the meeting point of Bingley, Morton, Ilkley and Burley moors. A wallside boundary stone is dated 1893.

**Through the gate you commence the return to the valley, a clear path heading down with the old wall. When a sturdy wall joins it, the path trends away from it to skirt Yellow Bog. After a steady slant you merge into a fine track, striding out left with distant views over the Aire Valley to Keighley. Beyond a gate it leaves the moor, passing a lone house to meet Otley Road at Drake Hill.**

Cross over and along Heights Lane just as far as a stile on the right. Descend half-left to a moist area preceding a fence-stile. A reedy corner leads to another stile, then head down a contrastingly lush, dry pasture to find a stile slightly left. East Morton is well seen across the valley of Morton Beck, a mirror image of one of the walk's early views. Cross the streamlet and head down, broadening into a green path through colourful terrain. On approaching Hill Top Lane (a concrete drive) turn down it to meet Carr Lane at the top of Micklethwaite, named from the Norse for 'big clearing'.

Descend the sloping upper green and down through the village. Attractive groupings include High Fold by the phone box, opposite the Methodist chapel. Further down the main street is Micklethwaite Grange on the right, dating from 1695. Legend suggests Cromwell fired on the original grange with cannon positioned on the Druid's Altar across the valley. Last but not least the lower green is reached. On one side sits the Manor House dated 1601, its mullions and transoms largely unaffected by division into separate dwellings. At the foot of the village a footway down Micklethwaite Lane brings a return to the canal at Micklethwaite Wharf. If time permits, a 10-minute walk left along the towpath leads to Five Rise Locks, showpiece of the Leeds-Liverpool Canal. Here, for over 200 years, five interlinking locks have lifted boats up a watery staircase - a fascinating spectacle and a fine piece of engineering.

*The Manor House, Micklethwaite*

## 7

# DOUBLER STONES

**START** *Holden Gate* **Grid ref. SE 065442**

**DISTANCE** *6 miles (9½ km)*

**ORDNANCE SURVEY MAPS**
*1:50,000*
*Landranger 104 - Leeds, Bradford & Harrogate*
*1:25,000*
*Explorer 297 - Lower Wharfedale & Washburn Valley **or***
*Explorer OL21 - South Pennines*

**ACCESS** *Leave the B6265 (old A650) at Riddlesden by Granby Lane traffic lights opposite East Riddlesden Hall. Climbing up it becomes Banks Lane, leaves Riddlesden and rises to a T-junction. Go left for half a mile to find a lay-by on the right just past Holden Gate.*

**Ⓢ From the lay-by head east towards Morton.** Sequestered in foliage, a forerunner of the attractive old house at Holden Gate served the deer preserves of the Cliffords of Skipton Castle. **Leave the road by an access track rising past a barn to serve both Rivock Edge plantation and a TV mast. Advance to the mast's enclosure and take a stile on the right, then advance beyond the enclosure to a stile in a crumbling wall. This admits to the large, unkempt tract of Rough Holden.** Up to the right, Rivock Edge maintains its dominance despite being humbled by alien trees. Scattered about its scarp are a number of cup and ring marked rocks.

**Go right and work steadily away from the wall, crossing an old fence.** Ahead now is a fine prospect of this ramble based on the valley of Holden Beck. **Maintain this line, a good little path forming to cross to a prominent wall-stile.** Here a good view back to the left takes in the two monuments on Earl Crag above Cowling, with Lancashire's Pendle Hill beyond. **Slant down to a fence-stile alongside a wall to overlook the tinkling stream of Dirk Hill Sike.**

34

Descend to cross the double-slab footbridge at an old sheepfold and from the bridle-gate behind, a green path winds round the foot of the spur to find a similar setting on a twin beck prior to their confluence. Rise to the wall above and go left to follow it to a corner stile. Remain on the wallside until crossing it at a solid stile before reaching Far Ghyll Grange. Slant up to a stile in the wall opposite, then up to a gate/stile. Ascend the field to a gate at the top. Rise with the wall to a stile in it, then make for the house at Black Pots, with a stile admitting onto a track.

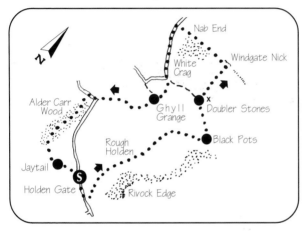

The track joined is the old bridle-road of Jerry Lane. Absorbing Black Pots' drive, turn left until it runs free above Doubler Stones Farm, and just before a bungalow turn up a thin path onto the moor. It runs below the weirdly weathered Doubler Stones, where a cup and ring marked rock can be inspected. Beyond a kissing-gate in an intervening fence the path is a delightful green trod in the heather, and meets a boundary wall running along the lofty crest of Rombalds Moor. Just a minute further comes the highlight of the walk's many features, arrival at Windgate Nick. This brings Wharfedale spectacularly into the scene, yet Airedale remains too.

Beneath your feet old delphs fall away, and the moor runs down from these old quarries to the farms of Addingham Moorside. Beyond it are the heights of Beamsley Beacon and Simon's Seat, with Barden Moor leading the eye to distant Buckden Pike and Great Whernside. The windfarm at Chelker Reservoir also draws the eye. Rombalds

Moor stretches far above Ilkley, while back over your shoulder Nab Hill rules the Pennine skyline above Oxenhope. **Turn left along the escarpment path, rejoining the wall at a stile which you ignore. As sunken ways turn downhill, remain on the wallside path to a corner stile. Go left on luxuriant turf outside an exposed plantation to Nab End.** A magnificent Airedale prospect is revealed: below are Silsden and Fishbeck Reservoir, with the silvery line of the Leeds-Liverpool Canal traced, and Earl Crag and a more distant Pendle Hill beyond. **The path drops past minor rocks onto Lightbank Lane.**

*At the Doubler Stones*

**Go left beneath White Crag until the road turns downhill, then take a gate in front onto Doubler Stones farm road. Leave at once by following the top side of a wall, an enclosed green way at the end falling to a farm road at Ghyll Grange.** A century ago visitors to the charms of Holden Beck found refreshment at the farm - though large parties required two days notice. **Entering the yard bear right after the house and out over a cattle-grid on the drive. At once take a track left, skirting the perimeter of the buildings to curve all the way round to a gate onto an enclosed track. Go right down its brief existence, then slant right down to an aqueduct over Holden Beck.** This is on the pipeline constructed by Bradford Corporation to carry

36

water from their Nidderdale reservoirs. **Descend to a footbridge and cobbled ford beneath, and turn downstream to a gate.**

*Deep within Holden Beck*

Ignore the track rising away and keep right on a little path through gorse above the confines of the beck, soon returning to its wooded environs at a stile. An absorbing path meanders downstream in colourful surroundings: at an early fork bear right. A minute later you pass a junction where you can double back down a flight of steps to peer into a mini-ravine secreting a hidden waterfall. The splendid path forges on, and soon rises out of the trees to merge with a bridle-path in a large pasture recently refreshed with young trees. This runs out to a gate onto a sharp corner of Holden Lane. Turning uphill would earn a more direct finish. **Turn down the road as far as a gate on the left, then cross a field bottom to experience the joys of Spring Crag and Alder Carr Woods.**

**Within a minute in the wood, take a clear fork up to the left, a brief climb preceding a long, level stride through beautiful woodland.** The super path follows the line of another Bradford aqueduct, from the reservoirs on Barden Moor. **At the far end, cross a track and rise just a few feet to a wall-stile into a field. Slant gently up the stony pasture on a grassy rake to a gate, then cross to another.** Looking back, Airedale is seen as comprehensively as ever. **Ascend the grassy track to Jaytail Farm, advancing straight on (left of the house) and rising out on a walled green way. Emerging into open country, bear right up to a stile onto the road at Holden Gate.**

# 8

# FARNHILL MOOR

**START** *Kildwick*      *Grid ref. SE 010458*

**DISTANCE** *4 miles (6½km)*

**ORDNANCE SURVEY MAPS**
*1:50,000*
*Landranger 104 - Leeds, Bradford & Harrogate*
*1:25,000*
*Explorer OL21 - South Pennines*

**ACCESS** *Start from the corner by the pub and church. Parking nearby, on the old road. Served by Keighley-Skipton buses.*

**⑤**   Only since the mid-1980s has Kildwick sat happily back from the bustle of the A629 through the Aire Valley, though it still catches sight and sound of heavy traffic bearing down on the nearby roundabout. Church, pub, cottages and bridge combine to create a delightful picture, the bridge being one of the oldest on the Aire. Rebuilt by the canons of Bolton in 1305 and since much widened, it is once again a place to gaze from the parapets without fear of being mown down. On the upstream side, two of the arches are pointed, while the other two are rounded. Opposite the *White Lion* is the old smithy.

**Take the road up the side of the church, going right past the old schoolhouse.** Note the stone tablet incorporated, and the date 1839. The parish church of St Andrew - known as the 'Lang Kirk o'Craven' - is a beautiful old building, with an imposing great tower and a lovely low-slung roof. Within is a good deal of carved oak, and remains of 10th century Anglo-Saxon crosses (two of which bear figures). Note also the resplendent Sir Robert de Styveton monument of 1307. Stiveton was the old name for Steeton, a village along the road towards Keighley. This corner collection is about all there is to Kildwick, for above the canal is the larger sister settlement of Farnhill.

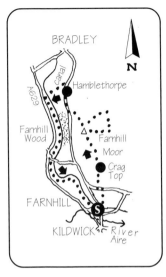

**Cross the arched bridge over an engaging stretch of the Leeds-Liverpool Canal.** Parson's Bridge is so named as it connects the church with the vicarage up the hill. **A flagged snicket rises to emerge onto a road just yards from Kildwick Hall, meriting a glance through the gate just along to the right.** This 17th century manor house displays an irregular gabled front, with mullioned and transomed windows. Lions guard the gates, while a colourful coat of arms sits above the door. After a spell as a restaurant it has reverted to a private dwelling. Half a mile further along the road, Kildwick Grange hamlet was originally a grange of Bolton Priory.

The route, meanwhile, goes left a short way, soon leaving the road by a path that rises onto the edge of Farnhill Moor. A choice of paths climb to the farm at Crag Top, and through a gate to its left the main body of the moor is underfoot. The most populous path curves above old quarries to the waiting Jubilee Tower on the skyline.

*Onto Farnhill Moor, at Crag Top*

Locally known as Farnhill Pinnacle, this 12ft high monument supports a stone carved cross bearing the initials VR, and a rose, shamrock and thistle. It was erected in 1887 to commemorate the Golden Jubilee of Queen Victoria. Words painstakingly carved on an adjacent stone explain that it was restored on the occasion of the Silver Jubilee of King George V, May 6th 1935. Also integral to the stone is a watering hole much favoured by the many canines that are exercised here.

*The big cairn, Farnhill Moor*

Alongside the stone is a seat from which to survey the outstanding Airedale vista. Across the valley is the old mill village of Cononley, while meandering below is a good length of the canal: down-dale Earl Crag and its monuments patrol the skyline, while beyond Skipton the peaks of Flasby Fell are prominent.

**For an essential perambulation of this pocket moor, turn along the thin path east to a similarly intriguing pointed beacon, a skilfully**

**constructed edifice. Continue past it to a crossroads of paths. Turn left to rise to the wall just alongside Tewit Mire, then left again with it.** Over the wall on Low Bradley Moor, is a 200ft long Neolithic long barrow. When excavated it revealed a stone cist containing bones, some of which were burnt. Nearer, at 833ft/254m on the very moortop of Black Hill, is a round barrow 100ft in diameter. **The path, meanwhile, soon swings away to be drawn back to the tower.**

**This time take a path north, commencing a descent of the moor into trees, and running on to join a road at the far corner. Go right for a few minutes, then just past Hamblethorpe Farm on the left, take a stile in the wall. A green track winds down the field to a gate, through which turn down the fieldside to cross Hamblethorpe swing-bridge on the canal.** Alongside is a modern memorial to seven Polish airmen whose Wellington bomber perished nearby in 1943. **Turn left along the towpath to return all the way to Kildwick.** Features en route are many: verdant Farnhill Woods with an awesome bluebell carpet in May; views back to the monument; Farnhill Bridge; a canal milestone indicating 25¼ to Leeds and 102 to Liverpool; and, imposingly across a loop of the canal, Farnhill Hall. Its very austere appearance is emphasised by dark turrets peering through the trees: parts date back to the 14th century when it offered refuge from marauding Scots. **Near the end Farnhill's array of canalside buildings are on parade before the canal crosses the village street on an aqueduct to return to Parson's Bridge.**

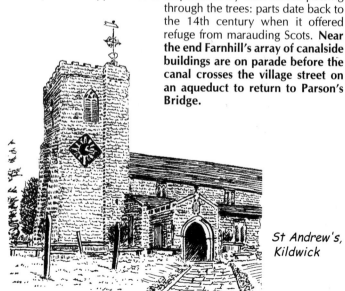

*St Andrew's, Kildwick*

# 9

# SKIPTON MOOR

**START** Bradley          Grid ref. SE 000482

**DISTANCE** 6 miles (9½ km)

### ORDNANCE SURVEY MAPS
1:50,000
Landranger 103 - Blackburn & Burnley
Landranger 104 - Leeds, Bradford & Harrogate
1:25,000
Explorer OL21 - South Pennines

**ACCESS** Start from the canal swing bridge on the road into the village; car park alongside. Regular bus service on the main road.

**⑤ From the canal bridge head up the lane past the sports field into the village, and at a T-junction by the shop use a snicket alongside the Methodist church.** Though the nucleus of the village is actually Low Bradley in deference to the farming hamlet of High Bradley high on the flanks of the Standard, in practise the whole place is simply Bradley. Village pub is the welcoming *Slaters Arms*. **Emerging onto a lane through a small modern development, turn left to the imposing Old Hall.** It bears a 1678 datestone, and forms a magnificent front to a working farm. Just back along the road to the right is the less obvious yet similarly impressive College House.

**Left of the hall a snicket emerges into a field, from a stile at the end you face renovated Ghyll Farm. Slant right to a small gate in the hedge above, descending steps to the top of the garden. From a gate on the right ascend a large field tapering to a gate at the top. Bear left to ascend by lovely North Beck, over an intervening wall-stile to a gate at the top.** With gorse in flower the hollow on your left is a riot of colour. **Through it go left onto a firmer track, rising to absorb Lower House Farm drive then up to Higher House. Just beyond, in an unkempt little enclosure, use a wall-stile at the top to bear left on the wallside track, crossing to a stile between adjacent gates.**

Head up the fieldside to a small barn, then bear left up to the top corner: the left-hand of two stiles admits to a tract of rough pasture. By now you can savour massive views over the Aire Valley to the long skyline of the South Pennines, featuring Boulsworth Hill and Pinhaw, beyond which Parlick makes a shapely cone on the Bowland moors.

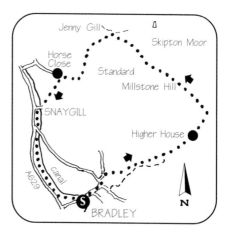

**Slant up once more to a stile in a kink in the top wall. A thin path maintains the line up a tussocky pasture to the boulders on Millstone Hill.** This reveals the bog of Black Sike, and the highest point of the Standard across to the left, with a stony edge - Standard Crag - beyond the marsh. **Strike a bee-line for the distant wall-corner left of the marsh, evading its excesses by crossing the outflow. When a wall comes up from the left, easier going brings arrival at a stile in the corner, on the Standard.** This is a stunning moment, with a wondrous prospect of the Aire Gap beyond the moor, and a bird's-eye view of Skipton town: beyond are the hills of Craven. Prominent across to the right is the summit of Skipton Moor, at 1224ft/373m.

*Standard Crag from Millstone Hill*

A sunken way now winds down in the Skipton direction. Beyond the head of a marshy area fork left to a stile by a wall corner. Just to the right the path continues down, and when it forks at a few reeds again bear left, a grassy way slanting back to the wall to reach a stile in it just short of a wall corner. From it bear gently away from the wall, a broad grass track passing above boulders before dropping to a gate/stile in a wall below. Slant left down the field (woodland on the map!) to find a wall-stile just above a gate in the bottom corner. Entering the moist, wooded environs of Cawder Gill, turn down the near side, a track forming to drop to a gate/stile back out into a field. Beyond a wall-corner advance to a drive just short of Cawder Hall. Go down this track to the main drive to the hall. Just beyond it, level with Horse Close Farm, pass through a small gate on the left to access a stile in the wall corner. Ahead is civilisation in the form of a modern hotel, industrial estate and main road.

Bear right down the field, round the base of a knoll to find a wall-stile. A path shadows a hummocky crest to squeeze through a snicket in the bottom corner onto a lane at Snaygill swing bridge (Low Snaygill on maps). Cross the canal and turn left on the towpath for a long, easy final mile. The *Bay Horse* pub is passed before reaching Snaygill Bridge and its multitude of colourful boats. The noise of the parallel road is escaped by swinging back towards Bradley, a very pleasant return to the village. Towards the end a milestone advises the distances to Leeds (27¼) and Liverpool (100).

Bradley Old Hall

44

## 10

# BOLTON ABBEY

**START** *Draughton*    *Grid ref. SE 038522*

**DISTANCE** *7½ miles (12km)*

### ORDNANCE SURVEY MAPS
*1:50,000*
*Landranger 104 - Leeds, Bradford & Harrogate*
*1:25,000*
*Explorer OL2 - Yorkshire Dales South/West*

***ACCESS*** *Start from the top end of the village just off the A65. Parking places on the sidelined old road. Served by Ilkley-Skipton bus.*

**S** Unassuming Draughton is a delightful village featuring lovely stone cottages and colourful gardens. It was by-passed in 1992, giving the villagers a good chance of getting to the Post office and back in one piece (before it closed in 2008). Some decades ago the *Matchless Inn* stood on the old main road, just above Draughton Quarry where contorted limestone is exposed. The village street descends from a sloping green where an old Bolton Abbey/Addingham guidepost stands outside a house. **Descend the street through the village, all the way to the A59 at Draughton Bottom.**

En route, note first the stocks outside the modest little church of St Augustine (1897), and the 17th century Manor House on the left part way down. Camouflaged by hedges enough is seen of this long, low building to appreciate its character. A little further is the modest Draughton Hall. While crossing the railway bridge at Draughton Bottom consider that through the efforts of enthusiasts trains are steaming below again: the Embsay & Bolton Abbey Steam Railway has successfully extended their preserved line from Embsay to create a new station on the old site at Bolton Abbey, on this track that originally linked Skipton with Ilkley.

Beyond Prior's Bridge cross the A59 with care to a stile just yards to the left, then cross a tiny footbridge to rise slightly left up the field. On a brow, a barn on the skyline is key to a stile to its right. Cross the field to a stile onto a green way in Halton East. Cross straight over onto a short-lived way to emerge between farm buildings onto the road through the hamlet. Along to the left beyond the phone box and tiny green is the 17th century Old Hall: visible is the east front with its intricate mullioned and transomed windows.

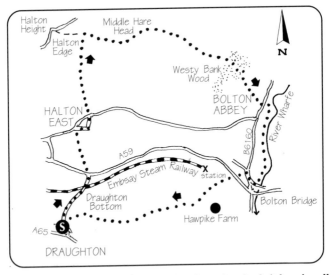

Go right, noting a paved section of path under the left-hand wall, backed by attractive cottages. At the end the road turns sharp left to a T-junction. Take the right-hand of two gates in front and head off with the wall through two fields, the second outside a slender plantation to a stile at the end. Entering rough pasture, a path rises to a stile in the opposite corner, then climb by the wall to emerge onto heathery Hare Head Side. The path quickly rises to the brow, meeting a broad grassy path on the summit of the walk. This is a supreme moment, a stunning panorama dominated by moorland. The massif of Barden Moor is the main feature, with Lower Barden Reservoir prominent. Far below is the Wharfe meandering down from Appletreewick, with Earl Seat and Simon's Seat rising behind, and further updale the broad shoulders of Great Whernside.

The path you join was immortalised by Wordsworth in his poem *The White Doe of Rylstone*. The story of the ill-fated Nortons of Rylstone tells of a widow undertaking the trek over Barden Moor to visit her husband's grave at the priory: the pet deer that accompanied her continued the journeys even after her death.

*The Old Hall, Halton East*

**Follow the White Doe path right through a gate to run in style over Middle Hare Head.** A few stones on the crest call for a pause to locate Barden Tower in the trees below. Much of lower Wharfedale is now in the scene, with Ilkley in a bowl of moorland. Directly opposite, the Valley of Desolation strikes deep into Barden Fell.

**The path drops to follow a wall down for some time until signalled through a gate in it. Striking directly away across a large pasture, it crosses a more distinct track at some water tanks. Your fainter way then slants down across another clear track to an intervening wall, then more directly down to a gate into Westy Bank Wood.** The wood hosts an enchanting springtime display of bluebells. **The good path turns right almost at once, then forks left. Winding down, it zigzags left then right to leave the foot of the wood. Cross to the left-hand of two gates in a corner, then head away outside tree-fringed ponds, continuing to a gate beyond. Bear left on the access track which drops onto the road opposite Bolton Hall.** Only now does Bolton Priory appear past the impressively castellated hall. **Either go right under the arch (an 18th century aqueduct) and then left through the 'Hole in the Wall' alongside a tearoom; or left along the road to enter the priory grounds through the churchyard.**

Bolton Priory (the Abbey name applies only to the village) was founded in 1151 by Alice de Romille, whose mother had endowed a priory for Augustinian canons at Embsay before they moved here.

The nave was spared at the Dissolution, and remains to this day the parish church adjoining the evocative priory ruins. Along with the surrounding moors, this whole area is part of the estate of the Duke of Devonshire. Other buildings of interest include Bolton Hall, west of the church, which incorporates the 14th century priory gatehouse. Alongside is the vicarage, while up on the road is a magnificent old tithe barn. At the main car park is a Post office/shop and WC.

**From the priory trace the Wharfe downstream to Bolton Bridge. Don't cross it but turn right on the old road to join the B6160 by an old milestone, and bear right past a tearoom to the *Devonshire Arms*. Cross to a gate accessing the old road, and head off just a short way along it before taking a stile on the left. Descend steps and cross the field to a footbridge on a tiny stream, then cross to join a sunken path, turning right on it to the 1994 Bolton Bridge by-pass in a cutting. Once across (with care), a path runs to a gate, then climb the field to a bridge above the overgrown railway.**

Ascend the wallside on a splendid sunken pathway - a carved stone marks Bradford Corporation's Nidd aqueduct - as far as a sharp

bend. Haw Pike is prominent up to the left. A path cuts out the bend by rising to a gate, and from it contour right across to a corner gate just past a spring. Head away with the wall on your left now, curving round to a gate to remain on the same side of the wall. At the next gate, in the very corner, veer away from the wall, using the isolated house at Haynholme on the slope opposite as a guide. A descent finds a stone slab bridge over Banks Gill, from where a wallside path rises to a gate. Join Haynholme's drive which has over-laid a fine green way, and it leads out to enter Draughton alongside the village hall.

*Bolton Priory*

## ( 11 )
# ROMBALDS WAY

**START** *Addingham*          *Grid ref. SE 084496*

**FINISH** *Skipton*          **DISTANCE** *6 miles (9½ km)*

**ORDNANCE SURVEY MAPS**
*1:50,000*
*Landranger 104 - Leeds, Bradford & Harrogate*
*1:25,000*
*Explorer OL2 - Yorkshire Dales South/West*
*Explorer 297 - Lower Wharfedale & Washburn Valley*
*(could manage with either one of these)*

**ACCESS** *A regular bus service links Addingham and Skipton, giving an ideal opportunity to enjoy a naturally linear walk. The parish churches make appropriate termini - Addingham's is at the very foot of the village, just above the river. The walk can however be picked up at any point on the Main Street, where buses will deposit you from a Skipton start.*

**S** *Rombalds* Way is the name accorded to this section of what was a prehistoric trade route between Ireland and the Continent, taking advantage of the Aire Gap to breach the Pennine Chain. It has since been used as a Roman road linking Ribchester to York via Ilkley, and as a coach road between Addingham and Skipton before the easier line of the motor road was carved. Before departing the lovely environs of St Peter's church, look inside to find a well-preserved Saxon cross (illustrated in WALK 12), a fine oak roof, and much evidence of the Thompson workshops of Kilburn.

**Leave the church grounds just to the right of the drive, by a tiny arched bridge that squeezes a footpath between houses onto North Street. Go left a few yards then quickly right along Church Street to gain the foot of Main Street. Turn up it** to appreciate its earlier name of Long Addingham. Shops, pubs and attractive dwellings line the street, which though by-passed in 1991 still sees ample traffic.

*Milestone on Draughton Height*

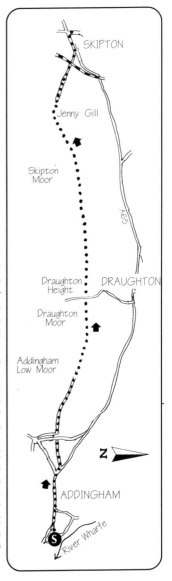

At the top, where the Keighley road turns off, continue a little further past the *Craven Heifer* then strike up Moor Lane. Though split by the by-pass pedestrian use remains, so cross the new road with care to continue up the hill. Running generally straight it stays surfaced for a considerable time, ever climbing and serving several farms and houses. The views widen all the while, with Beamsley Beacon and Simon's Seat over to the right, and the Chelker windfarm sails much nearer. As it levels out it undulates on to finally become a rough track, and at a gate into a field is suddenly surprisingly faint. Maintain a direct line up a sketchy embanked trackway to a gate at the top, beyond which the top of a pasture is crossed to a gate onto Draughton Moor.

At this point the delights of Barden Moor, and to its left, Flasby Fell overtopped by the heights beyond Malhamdale come into view. Down to the right, meanwhile, is probably the best view of Chelker Reservoir, both dammed ends being conspicuous - on the face of it a strange place to gather water. Its windfarm is alongside, the whole being backed by great sweeps of moorland, with Great Whernside topping the skyline high up Wharfedale.

**A lovely section ensues alongside heathery Draughton Moor, running on to meet the minor road from Silsden over to Draughton.** Not to be missed here is an old milestone, carved with the distances to Skipton, Addingham, Draughton, and Silsden: note how the longer names over-run. **Cross straight over and a grand track makes light work of the reedy surrounds of Draughton Height. It runs on by the dense Back Plantation before a damper section.** Here enjoy a look down the ravine of Potters Gill just past the plantation. All the time there is a panorama of increasing grandeur over to the wilder heights of Barden Moor and more distant Dales scenery: the unsightly Haw Quarry is dwarfed by the scale of the moor. On your left Skipton Moor extends a long way, gaining steepness as the old road marches on: capacious verges indicate the former importance of this route.

**Eventually the way falls through attractive woodland to drop more steeply past an old quarry to the terminus of Shortbank Road on the outskirts of Skipton.** As the road forges on into town, an early item of exceptional interest is the old toll house. **Keep on, passing under a railway bridge and, at the end, bear left along Newmarket Street to emerge onto the High Street. Go left for the bus station and then quickly right (Broughton Road) for the rail station.**

*The old tollhouse,
Shortbank Road,
Skipton*

Skipton occupies a strategic location in the Aire Gap, a low-level route through the Pennines used for trade and military purposes, and in more recent centuries exploited by both canal and rail. The broad High Street, with its spacious setts up either side, is a lively scene on market days (Monday, Wednesday, Friday, Saturday) when stalls squeeze cheek by jowl in front of the shops. Pride of place goes to the parish church at the head of the street. 14th century features include part of the tower. Damaged during the Civil War, the church, like the castle, was repaired by Lady Anne Clifford. Of note are the rood screen of 1533, the great oak beams of the medieval roof, and the Clifford tombs. That of George, the Third Earl (1605) is richly decorated with armorial bearings of the Clifford line.

Mention of the Cliffords leads to Skipton's finest building, its well-preserved castle. Open to visitors, it is entered through an enormous 14th century gatehouse. The castle dates from Norman times, being founded by the de Romilles, coming into the Cliffords' possession in 1309, when it was largely rebuilt. For 3½ centuries it was the home of the powerful Cliffords. George, 13th Lord and 3rd Earl, was a sea captain who helped overcome the Armada, while his remarkable daughter Anne, the last Clifford, still journeyed between her various castles - including Brougham and Appleby, in Westmorland - at a ripe old age to restore and maintain them. A short excursion around the back of the castle into Skipton Woods, by crossing Mill Bridge over Eller Beck, leads by way of three parallel watercourses - the beck, the Springs Branch of the canal (which carried quarried stone) and a mill-cut, to view the castle's impregnable northern face. Also worth visiting is the Craven Museum, while the Leeds-Liverpool Canal glides through the heart of town.

*Gatehouse,
Skipton
Castle*

# CHELKER RESERVOIR

(12)

**START** *Addingham*        *Grid ref.  SE 077498*

**DISTANCE** *5½ miles (9km)*

**ORDNANCE SURVEY MAPS**
*1:50,000*
*Landranger 104 - Leeds, Bradford & Harrogate*
*1:25,000*
*Explorer 297 - Lower Wharfedale & Washburn Valley*

**ACCESS** *Start at the foot of Main Street, in the vicinity of the Fleece pub. Served by Keighley-Ilkley and Skipton-Ilkley buses.*

**S** Addingham - formerly Long Addingham - was the scene, in 1826, of a thousand-strong Luddite riot, an abortive attempt to break into the mill to smash powerlooms. Today little industry remains in what was the first major mill settlement on the Wharfe. Despite the 1991 by-pass, Addingham's main street retains much of its bustle, and manages to support five pubs and numerous shops. **From Main Street turn towards Ilkley, and near the foot of the village go left along Church Street to a junction with North Street. Straight ahead a gap gives access to the grounds of St Peter's church.** Of particular interest are its splendid oak roof, preserved Saxon cross, and examples of the mouse trademark of the famous Kilburn workshops.

**The route turns left along North Street before a path descends to a suspension footbridge over the Wharfe. Don't cross but turn upstream on a path keeping with the river at a fork. High Mill - now modern homes - soon deflects you briefly from the river, through its courtyard and ahead to a drive into a caravan park: a path returns you to the Wharfe alongside a weir. The river now leads unfailingly up-dale, though after a couple of fields the way is temporarily forced up above a steep, wooded bank. After further delightful riverbank rambling another wooded bank intervenes.**

**This time a stile leads into trees to skirt a house to join the B6160. Cross to a small gate accessing to the Friends' Meeting House.** This splendid old Quaker building is dated 1689. **Behind it join the drive to Lobwood House. Bear left around the buildings and along the firm track past stables to an old rail underpass.** The Skipton-Ilkley line closed in 1965, a sad loss as it linked stations that remain active.

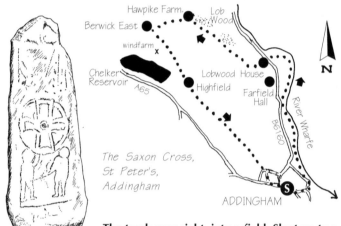

The Saxon Cross,
St Peter's,
Addingham

**The track runs right, into a field. Slant up to a gate from where a track maintains the slant, locating a stile above Eller Carr Wood. Now more level, maintain the same line towards a stile above a slightly higher wood top.** The view has by now opened out, from Rombalds Moor down the valley, up past Beamsley Beacon, Bolton Bridge, Bolton Abbey, the Valley of Desolation, Simon's Seat, and the moors running up the head of Wharfedale to Great Whernside. **Contouring on above the trees Hawpike Farm appears as a guide ahead, and crossing towards it a gate and tiny stream are encountered before rising up an enclosure to a gate onto a farmyard track.**

Go left away from the buildings, passing right of a large, modern barn and back into fields. A bield on the brow above is the target, and a curving track winds up past this sheep shelter. On below the crest of Haw Pike (OS column at 827ft/252m) it slopes invitingly round towards white-walled Berwick East Farm. Here is a first sighting of Chelker Reservoir. **Pass through a gate alongside a house before the farm, then out along its drive. On merging with** a drive from the right, strike left on a fading path through young trees to a stile near the corner. Ascend the field to a stile in the top corner. An adjacent gatepost is inscribed 1817. **Head away with the wall along a broad ridge, with the reservoir more satisfactorily revealed behind the masts of the windfarm.** Erected in 1992, the area's first multi-mast site caused heated debate, being on the edge of a national park and visible from many notable viewpoints. Less controversial is the reservoir of 1858, a favourite haunt of birdlife.

**Cross to the other side of the wall at the end of the field, returning to the right side at a corner stile a short way beyond the next gate. Passing the last turbine, advance to a gate at the end, then cross a track to locate a stile in a dip, alongside a small embankment. Advance to Highfield Farm, using a gate left of the main buildings to enter the yard. Opposite the house take a gate on the left and cross to a gate onto Bracken Ghyll golf course. Advance straight on the edge of the course, passing Highfield House on the right. A little further the way runs past a stone shed down the centre of the course, maintaining the same line to leave by a stile at the bottom.**

**Continue down an inviting wooded avenue. Adjacent to the ruined barn of High Laithe, the path continues down parallel with an entirely overgrown sunken way. This remains a lovely course, passing through a stile and down again to one on the left before the bottom corner. With the now servicable lane of Long Riddings alongside, remain parallel until a wicket-gate at the very bottom gives entry to the lane. This runs on to join a road. Go left and then sharp right along Sugar Hill to re-enter Main Street alongside the old railway.**

*At Chelker Reservoir*

## 13

# WINDGATE NICK

**START** *Ilkley      Grid ref.  SE 112480*

**DISTANCE** *7½  miles (12km)*

**ORDNANCE SURVEY MAPS**
*1:50,000*
*Landranger 104 - Leeds, Bradford & Harrogate*
*1:25,000*
*Explorer 297 - Lower Wharfedale & Washburn Valley*

**ACCESS** *Start from the Old Bridge at the upstream end of the riverside park. Car parks, buses and rail station in the town centre.*

**S** Turning away from the former packhorse bridge, head up **Stockeld Road** between the *Ilkley Moor Vaults* and the Catholic church. **Cross over the main road and up Westville Road. Over a crossroads keep on to a T-junction, then right along spacious Grove Road.** Many of the more illustrious dwellings in this area were built for wealthy mill owners from Bradford and Leeds. On the right, the enormous mansion of Heathcote hides in the very heart of a strange suburbia. It was the work, in the early 1900s, of fashionable architect Sir Edwin Lutyens.

**Turn left at a crossroads with Victoria Avenue, and at the top continue up a snicket onto Queen's Drive at the foot of Panorama Woods, decorated with bluebells. Go right past the last of the houses below - now as Hollin Hall Drive - and as it swings up to the left keep straight on a level path into open country. At an old wall keep to the main, right-hand path, and with the sound of Heber's Ghyll in the trees ahead, drop down stone steps to a road. At once cross a bridge on the left and take a well-surfaced path rising into trees alongside Heber's Ghyll. The tumbling beck is re-crossed no less than six times during this steep woodland ascent, before arriving at the remains of a rest hut: paths to either side emerge onto the foot of the moor. Go right on the wallside path, through**

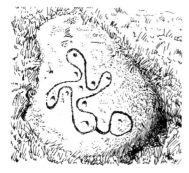

**a corner gate to slant up to a higher path along to the iron railings guarding the Swastika Stone on Woodhouse Crag.** Thought to date from the Bronze Age it resembles versions found in Scandinavia. The original is the less obvious carving on the main rock, that at the front a replica for ease of viewing.

*The Swastika Stone*

**The path now traces the crest of the well-defined if intermittent gritstone edge of Piper's Crag, rising ever gradually through stiles and by some windswept trees, after which a string of iron gates in intervening walls punctuate this classic march.** Enjoy super views over Addingham and Bolton Abbey to hazy heights up Wharfedale. Some of the more prominent boulders to your right bear cup and ring markings: abundant on these moors, they are further relics of Bronze Age times. **Shortly after the distinctive block of the isolated Noon Stone, the final interruption is a stile in an angled wall: the path now enjoys a short spell in the heather away from the edge.** Here is a brief opportunity to survey two major valleys, as Airedale appears over to the left, with the Bronte moors beyond Keighley and the Worth Valley and as far as the moors of Bowland. **Soon a cairn is reached signifying the path crossroads at Windgate Nick.**

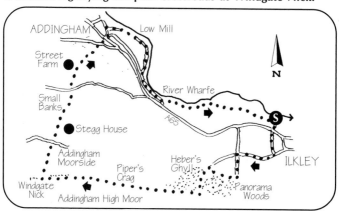

The moor-edge you have trodden is part of a prehistoric trade-route, possibly a major link between Ireland and the Continent. It was christened Rombalds Way by a local historian half a century ago. Your impending descent to the valley is also on historic trading lines, a packhorse link between the Aire Valley settlements and Addingham.

*Heber's Ghyll*

**Here, yards short of the edge's highest point, descend through the aptly-named Nick into a former quarry. Almost at once fork right on a path slanting below the cliffs, through a rash of stones to a stile in the wall. From a stile in the lower corner a wall leads down to Moorside Lane serving the scattered farms of Addingham Moorside. Cross straight over and down the Stegg House Farm drive: as it crosses a beck go left on a short way emerging into a field, then descend to the crest of a steeper bank. Drop left to a corner stile from where a pleasant, largely obvious way descends fields to a tiny slab bridge. Follow the wall rising left from it, up to a small gate and along a garden edge onto the road through Small Banks.**

**Just yards to the left a stile on the right resumes the descent, down a fieldside and across to a stile above a wooded bank. A stepped descent to a footbridge in a near-hidden valley leads to a gate up the other side.** Around this point you cross the line of the Roman road from Ilkley through the Aire Gap to Ribchester: just along to the left, Street Farm's name maintains the link. **Bear slightly right over open pasture to a gate in the bottom corner, where a stone bridge crosses the infilled course of the Ilkley-Skipton railway. Across, take a kissing-gate on the left to encounter the Addingham by-pass and cross with care. From an identical gate opposite drop to**

another, but without using it go right with the fence to the next such gate, then descend half-right to one at the bottom corner. This accesses the road into Addingham.

Cross and bear left onto Church Street, but quickly leave it by Low Mill Lane. An early gate offers a tempting diversion to the parish church. Set in a verdant corner where Town Beck gurgles under tiny arched bridges made for churchgoers, parts of St Peter's date from medieval times, while the nave sports a fine oak roof. A small Saxon cross is preserved showing two figures under a cross (see WALK 12). Seek also the 'mouse' carvings of the famous Kilburn workshops. Alongside is the imposing old rectory, an equally lovely scene where peacocks strut and ducks dabble in the stream.

*Churchgoers' bridge over Town Beck, Addingham*

At Low Mill Lane's demise you enter Low Mill Village, a tasteful enhancement of this old mill corner. Just across the weir on the river, Castleberg Scar is an Iron Age dwelling site. Keep straight on the access road to a T-junction, and turn left on the old road to Ilkley, with a golf course across the parallel Wharfe.

At the first opportunity branch left on a footpath into a riverside pasture. It continues on a wooded bank above the Wharfe, emerging at the end to abandon the river after crossing a tiny stream where a kingfisher startled me. The way now runs a clear course through the fields: after one field's-length it becomes enclosed, emerging to cross further fieldsides through old kissing-gates then across a field centre to reach a tennis club. Go right on its drive, keeping straight on a broad path when the road climbs away. At this point the Old Bridge appears just two minutes ahead.

# 14

# BUCK STONES

**START** Ilkley        Grid ref. SE 117471

**DISTANCE** 5½ miles (9km)

**ORDNANCE SURVEY MAPS**
1:50,000
Landranger 104 - Leeds, Bradford & Harrogate
1:25,000
Explorer 297 - Lower Wharfedale & Washburn Valley

**ACCESS** The walk is deemed to start from Darwin Gardens car park, immediately above the moorfoot cattle-grid at the top of Wells Road, which climbs steeply from the main shopping thoroughfare, The Grove. Railway station, buses and car parks in the town centre.

**⑤ Returning to Keighley Road, bear right along the base of the moor.** On your right is Wells House, built in 1856 as one of a number of hydropathic establishments catering for the demand for curing ailments by means of liberal contact with the cold waters that sprang from the moor (see WALK 15). **At a fork with Westwood Drive keep left to remain with the moor. Bridging Spicey Gill, the road turns to ascend alongside it.** Soon passed on your right is an old guidepost inscribed to Keighley and Ilkley, complete with carved hands. **A little further, as the road leaves the beck, a path heads into bracken on the left. Rising right at a fork, it climbs above the gill's deep confines to rejoin the now unsurfaced Keighley Road on a green knoll above the amphitheatre of Grainings Head.**

Cowper's Cross and Keighley Gate radio masts are on the skyline above, with Ilkley's resplendent setting below. **Unfit for ordinary motors, the road leads up and on towards Whetstone Gate (more commonly known as Keighley Gate). Two minutes before it, however, a path branches right to Cowper's Cross.** A cowper was a dealer or barterer, and it seems this was a market cross brought from elsewhere, later converted to a true cross.

**The Buck Stones are now seen close to hand, and a clear path continues away, running a splendid, level course to soon reach them.** First on the agenda are East Buck Stones, a fine group of boulders which at 1299ft/ 396m mark the highest point of the walk. Apart from excellent views up Wharfedale, they also enjoy a southerly panorama over Airedale.

**A path continues the short way to the watershed wall, where the similarly sited West Buck Stones hover over a pronounced escarpment.** These offer good shelter from a sudden shower, and similar sweeping views over the moor. Here you can also survey the vastness of the plantations that now cloak the hinterland of Rivock Edge, which only shows its true face to the Keighley side. Beyond the trees the Aire Valley leads the eye to the South Pennine landmarks of Earl Crag and Pinhaw Beacon, with the great whaleback of Pendle Hill, in Lancashire, beyond. Northwards are many peaks of the southern half of the Dales, with Buckden Pike and Great Whernside prominent.

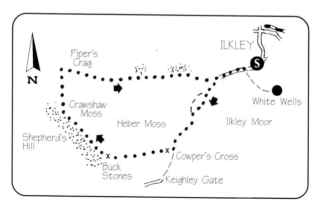

In the ensuing depression walkers have trodden a slightly drier course around Crawshaw Moss, returning to the wall to meet a pair of boundary stones just beyond a bend, on a minor knoll. The larger one is inscribed *WM 1842 ILB*. **Here a path strikes off across the heather moor, descending steadily past another dated boundary stone before commencing a sharper drop.** The panorama up Wharfedale is absolutely beautiful, looking over Addingham to Bolton Bridge, Bolton Abbey - the priory itself is easily discerned - Simon's Seat and Beamsley Beacon, though the wind turbines at Chelker Reservoir are an intrusion. **Slant left on the path down to a stile in a short length of wall, then down again to quickly meet an unmissable, popular path along the distinct Wharfedale edge.**

**Here turn right, encountering several gates and stiles on a super path with views to match, traversing above a host of minor outcrops including Piper's Crag to reach the famous Swastika Stone, guarded by iron railings on Woodhouse Crag.** Thought to date from Bronze Age times, it shares the characteristics of symbols found in Scandinavia. The main carving visible is a replica, the original being less discernible on the main rock, further back (illustrated in WALK 13). **The path runs on to slant down to cross Black Beck above the woods containing Heber's Ghyll. The way now becomes a broader pathway to return along the base of the moor to meet the road at Spicey Gill.** The return can be varied by eschewing the road in favour of various paths on the moor, possibly cutting across to visit White Wells, featured in WALK 15.

*The Buck Stones, looking across Wharfedale*

# 15

# DICK HUDSON'S

**START** *Ilkley*          *Grid ref.  SE 116478*

**DISTANCE** *8 miles (13km) (or 4 miles/6½km one-way only)*

**ORDNANCE SURVEY MAPS**
*1:50,000*
*Landranger 104 - Leeds, Bradford & Harrogate*
*1:25,000*
*Explorer 297 - Lower Wharfedale & Washburn Valley*

**ACCESS** *Start from the parish church in the centre of town. Car parks, bus stops and rail station nearby.*

This time-honoured packhorse and early tourist route provides an invigorating tramp across Ilkley Moor to a famous public house.

**S** **Commence at the doorway of All Saints parish church.** Though largely rebuilt in 1860, it has a tower around 500 years old and a doorway from the 13th century, but is best known for its Anglo-Saxon crosses. Dating from the 9th century, the tallest and most important bears a figure of Christ, with four figures on the reverse. Seek out also a well-preserved effigy of a 14th century knight, Adam de Middleton. The church covers part of the site of the Roman fort of Olicana, built around 79 AD. It sat on the trans-Pennine road from Ribchester to Tadcaster and York, which here crossed another road from Manchester to Aldborough, near Boroughbridge. Evidence is restricted to a small section of preserved wall. Also by the church is the 16th century Manor House, a museum of local historical interest.

**Head up Brook Street onto the main shopping thoroughfare of The Grove, then cross to the gardens of Wells Promenade. Here a path rises through charming surroundings onto Wells Road and up to the foot of Ilkley Moor. Directly above is White Wells: go left to a gate before the cattle-grid to locate the start of a surfaced path climbing to it.** This humble cottage is a monument to Ilkley's spa

**63**

days. In the mid-19th century large hydros were built for people to take of the therapeutic waters, but a century earlier Squire Middleton built White Wells as a bath-house to enable townsfolk to enjoy a dip in the pure moorland spring water. In the 1970s it was restored and is now a museum and visitor centre serving refreshments. Inside is a deep circular pool hollowed from the rock and fed by a cold mineral spring - no longer available for a plunge. Ilkley flourished as a spa town - the 'Malvern of the North' - and the Victorians revelled in the healing powers of its waters. By the turn of the century the fashion had passed, but by that time Ilkley was firmly on the tourist map. By the time you get here you'll enjoy magnificent views over the town to the bleaker moors opposite, and up the valley into the Dales.

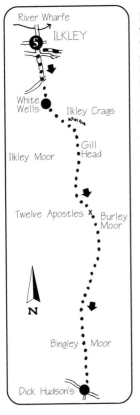

**Behind the cottage a stepped path climbs to join a broader one, running left to a fork below a plantation. Bear right up a stone staircase above the onset of Ilkley Crags.** The lower path running through the fascinating Rocky Valley is worth noting, possibly for inclusion in the return journey. **Just above the start of the crags the way eases and the real climbing is now complete. A sprawling cairn presides over a path crossroads as the *Dick Hudson's* path advances straight on up the moor.** Dramatic views over Ilkley and the valley are replaced with wilder moorland.

**Gill Head is crossed and the path features boardwalks and stone flags as it runs up to the prominent boundary stoop of Lanshaw Lad.** Inscribed with several sets of initials and the year 1833, the Lad delineates the division between Ilkley and Burley Moors, and also marks a splendid viewpoint. Landmarks include Barden Moor, Buckden Pike, Great Whernside, Beamsley Beacon, Round Hill, Menwith Hill, Almscliff Crag, the Hambleton Hills on the North York Moors, and Otley Chevin.

**Having reached its zenith the path runs on two minutes further to the Twelve Apostles.** Presumed to be of Bronze Age origin like so many moorland relics, its dozen stones form a circle 50 feet in diameter. The site overlooks both Wharfedale and Airedale, and across to man's more intrusive ornaments on Menwith Hill. **The path resumes in style, slowly descending to a large guidepost inscribed to Eldwick, Saltaire, Bingley and Ilkley, then on to a gate. Forging on it passes another guidepost and enjoys a paved spell, rising to a small gate and along to a sunken drop between old walls to *Dick Hudson's*.**

The *Fleece* at High Eldwick has been known for more than a century as Dick Hudson's in deference to its famous proprietor for 30 years from 1850, a period that was perhaps its heyday. Victorian and Edwardian workers made this a place of pilgrimage, seeking refuge from the urban grime. Easter holiday weekend was the busiest of times, when they would come in their hordes via Bingley and Saltaire to stride out for the moors, often crossing to Ilkley and back in the day: inevitable refreshment breaks were at Dick's, usually on both legs of the journey. The inn served travellers from early morning to late at night, most popular fare being the Yorkshire speciality, ham and egg teas. Only in relatively recent times, with widespread car ownership, has the practise diminished, though the trek across the moor to or from the inn has lost little of its appeal. The present building dates from around 1900, though its predecessors would have served the packhorse trade on this moorland route. It was here also that the author and his intended pulled a few thousand pints of Yorkshire ale in order to assemble a deposit for their first house. **If your desire for sustenance has been too heavily fulfilled, you don't have to walk back: simply turn down the Bingley road to the bus terminus just above Eldwick. Or, you might reverse WALK 5's journey to Saltaire via Shipley Glen, then return to Ilkley by rail.**

*Dick Hudson's*

# 16

# DENTON & MIDDLETON

**START** *Ilkley*     *Grid ref. SE 112480*

**DISTANCE** *6 miles (9½ km)*

**ORDNANCE SURVEY MAPS**
*1:50,000*
*Landranger 104 - Leeds, Bradford & Harrogate*
*1:25,000*
*Explorer 297 - Lower Wharfedale & Washburn Valley*

**ACCESS** *Start from the Old Bridge, just upstream from the main road bridge. Car parks, buses and railway station in the town centre.*

Originally serving the packhorse trade, the Old Bridge was rebuilt after the great flood of 1673 that swept away many of the Wharfe's bridges. Happily it has long been left to be enjoyed by pedestrians, and the walk concludes by crossing it.

**❸Follow the Wharfe downstream past the *Riverside Hotel*, rowing boats and children's playground.** These broad green spaces are the townsfolk's memorial to their fallen in World War Two. Enjoy also a silhouette of the Cow and Calf Rocks on the skyline before **taking advantage of an underpass below the road bridge.** This was opened in 1904, replacing a ferry that supplemented the Old Bridge. **Continue downstream on this still urban path nudged by suburbia onto a quieter section between cemetery and river to a suspension footbridge high above the Wharfe.** This affords a good view back over the town to the terraces of Rombalds Moor.

**Cross to the Denton road under Stubham Wood and resume downstream, using some verges parallel with the Wharfe, passing a drive to the chalets of the Nell Bank Centre, and a field where the local riding club holds regular shows. Just beyond, at a stile on the left, cross to the far corner of a field, then along a fieldside below trees to a kissing-gate onto Carters Lane.**

**Take the drive to Beckfoot Farm opposite. Crossing the bridge on Bow Beck into the yard, go straight ahead past the farmhouse garden.** A relocated Middleton/Denton boundary stone stands by the garden wall. **Turn left outside the wall along a narrow enclosure to a small gate in the boundary wall.** At this original site of the stone, escape into North Yorkshire, and a sylvan paradise. **Cross and bear right outside a lovely section of West Park Wood. Beyond two stiles a track out of the wood runs on through two further fields to join a road. Turn up its leafy course into the tiny village of Denton.**

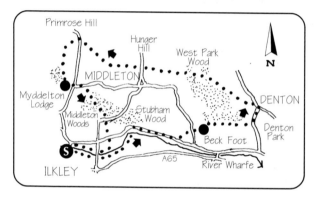

Directly ahead is the old school - note the bell in situ. **Your departure is by the road left.** Along to the right, however, past Home Farm, is the drive to Denton Hall. In 1515 the old hall became, for around 200 years, home of one of Yorkshire's more famous families, when Sir William Fairfax married a daughter of the Thwaites family, who came over with the Conqueror. Sir - later Lord - Thomas 'Black Tom' Fairfax was a major figure in the Civil War, a soldier who led the Parliamentarian forces in numerous clashes: greatest was the Battle of Marston Moor in 1644. The present hall dates from around 1770: designed by the renowned John Carr of York, it is currently in educational use. While there are no rights of way through the grounds, you can glimpse something of the great scale of things by a wander on by the church. In any case, St Helen's church is worth a visit in its own right. By the same architect and entirely unspoilt, it dates from 1776 and was a private chapel until becoming the parish church in 1867. It enjoys a sequestered rural setting, and possesses a rare stained glass window removed from the old hall. If the door should be locked a key can be obtained locally.

Back at the junction head away to quickly find a stile onto a short-lived enclosed track on the left, below a duckpond. At the end advance with a fence to the top of West Park Wood. A stile keeps you out of the trees, running along the top to find one conceding access into the far end of the wood. Path and footbridge combine to see you rapidly back out. The croak of a pheasant conveys the atmosphere of a typical country estate, and certainly Denton's seems to be an active one. Cross a field almost enveloped by woodland to another stile inevitably into the trees, and a path descends to a footbridge over Bow Beck and steeply up the bank.

Bearing right at the top the path runs through the wood-edge, with the grounds of the old Middleton Hospital to the left. On leaving the trees at a stile the way traces a fence through further stiles to steps down to a tiny footbridge, then cross to a stile onto Hunger Hill Lane. Cross to a stile opposite and head past a house: a series of step-stiles escape a modern barn to continue away with a wall. From a stile at the end forge on with a winding wall, and towards the end of this large field slant up to a gateway opposite. During this spell savour the widest views yet, with the entire spread of Rombalds Moor over to your left.

Continue up to a fence-stile and rise again to the opposite corner to emerge via a stile onto a bend of Hardings Lane at Primrose Hill. This summit of the walk is an historic spot: the ascending road is on the line of the Roman road from Ilkley to Boroughbridge, and the track known as Parkes Lane traces its course onto the moor. Cross to a gate opposite and head down the fieldside. Past the top of a plantation pass through a gate onto a track, then turn left on it through a gate in a wall. It descends pleasantly to a wood edge and joins a drive. Immersed in woodland to the right is Calvary, a special place in the grounds of Myddelton Lodge (now known as Myddelton Grange). Created around 1850, carved stones representing the Stations of the Cross line a path to a grotto: a beautiful, peaceful location.

*At Myddelton Lodge*

**The drive descends past cottages to swing left back onto Hardings Lane.** Myddelton Lodge is a pastoral centre of the Roman Catholic Diocese of Leeds. It was rebuilt around 1600 by William Middleton, a member of one of the oldest families in the county. Middletons resided here as influential Catholics until the estate was passed to the church. The chapel was built in 1854, and for 50 years Ilkley folk climbed the hill to worship until a church was built in the town. The imposing house is a tall gritstone building sporting mullioned and transomed windows. Modern buildings alongside help fulfil its modern-day role, and various statues add to its charm. Just down Hardings Lane stood the crucifixion scene illustrated.

**On Hardings Lane, turn left to a junction, noting an old milestone here: go right along the Middleton lane. Past a lone house take a stile and slant left down the field to a stile into Middleton Woods.** Springtime bluebells decorate this popular spot. **An immediate fork is the first of many twists and turns: go right, then quickly left at another fork to descend a little before running left to a junction just short of a small clearing. Turn right down a flight of stone steps, then left again over a tiny footbridge just beyond a crossroads with a thinner path. A slight kink left crosses a wooden way over moist ground, just past which is a major fork: keep right, dropping down a finger of woodland between houses to emerge via hollies onto a suburban avenue.**

**Go briefly left to descend to playing fields at the open air pool.** Suddenly you're back in the thick of things! On a nice day there'll be people slurping ice cream and picnicking amongst numerous sporting attractions. **Go past the pool to cross a road, on past the rugby ground to the riverbank. Go right to the new bridge (no tunnel on this bank) to return by the Wharfe to the more endearing Old Bridge.**

*St Helen's, Denton*

## 17

# BEAMSLEY BEACON

**START** Hazlewood        Grid ref. SE 094540

**DISTANCE** 7½ miles (12km)

**ORDNANCE SURVEY MAPS**
1:50,000
Landranger 104 - Leeds, Bradford & Harrogate
1:25,000
Explorer OL2 - Yorkshire Dales South/West **or**
Explorer 297 - Lower Wharfedale & Washburn Valley

**ACCESS** *On its climb from Beamsley to Blubberhouses Moor the A59 has seen numerous improvements to by-pass farming hamlets, leaving many sidelined sections of road. The start is at Hill End, where a lengthy section of old road returns to the main road some 200 yards below a parking area that hosts a much patronised snack bar: just over the bridge is a large lay-by on the wide, deserted road.*

**❺ Return to the main road and cross with care.** At once absorb the colourful valley of Kex Beck tumbling from the moors, while viewing the bulk of Beamsley Beacon ahead. **From a gate a surfaced track transforms into an unspoilt green way dropping to a gate accessing a wooden footbridge on the beck. Turning downstream the thin path leaves the beck to rise away with a wall to Low Howgill Farm.** High above is a thrusting, bouldery edge.

**Absorbing Low Howgill's drive, the way runs above Howgill Side and on to Ling Chapel Farm. As its drive arrives to join yours, take a grassy path slanting up the moor to gain the unenclosed Beamsley-Langbar road near its crest. Almost without setting foot on it a track goes left by a wall. When it heads across the moor climb with the wall to meet the direct - and return - path on the brow. Turn to scale it, gaining the defined northern edge for a wonderful ascent through heather, easing out as Beamsley Beacon's summit cairn appears.**

This is a well-blazed trail, being a perfect mini-mountain for young 'uns. At 1289ft/393m an OS column is dwarfed by a huge pile of stones, with shelters adjacent and some outcrops just beyond. The moorland panorama includes, anti-clockwise from the north-east: Kex Gill Moor, Rocking Moor, Hazlewood Moor, Simon's Seat, Earl Seat, Barden Moor, Flasby Fell, Skipton Moor, Rombalds Moor, Otley Chevin and back to Blubberhouses Moor. Wharfedale occupies the valley floor, with March Ghyll Reservoir prominent nearby, though finest feature is the bird's-eye view over today's agenda.

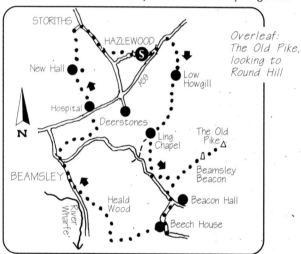

*Overleaf:*
*The Old Pike,*
*looking to*
*Round Hill*

**Appraising the view it becomes apparent there is higher ground five minutes along the ridge, and the path runs on to the Old Pike.** At 1312ft/400m its top is marked by a shelter among a group of rocks in the heather. **Return over the Beacon Hall down to the road top. Turn left towards the grounds of Beacon Hall and sharp right down to the scattered community of Langbar. After a steep drop to an open area the road swings left again, still descending. At the next farm, Beech House, turn right into its yard. Past the house go right above a row of cattle sheds to emerge into a field. Remaining with the wall above, make for a gate just above a small barn. Astride the national park boundary, you'll probably find it won't budge. Pass the barn in this garden edge, bearing left to a gate into a field.** The ha-hà of adjacent and attractive-looking Currer Hall no doubt enhances its view across to Rombalds Moor.

Slant down the field, crossing an intervening stile to a kissing-gate in the corner. Descend to cross a stile in the adjacent wall then cross to a corner stile. Pass through a line of trees to a wood below a barn, then follow its perimeter fence down to the left. A springtime carpet of bluebells illuminates the wood edges. **Adhere to the fence around the foot of Heald Wood to a stile in a wall below, then turn back up to the wood bottom. Towards the end is an invisible path junction: bear left down to a gate where fence and wall meet, and on to a duplicate situation below. Ignore the track through this gate and cross the field to a ladder-stile in the facing wall. Within yards a grassy track materialises to run below a plantation and on to a gate onto Lowfield Lane.**

**Turn right into the tiny village of Beamsley. Crossing Kex Beck, note the former mill upstream. Fifty yards past the mill drive turn opposite a Victorian postbox into Hardy Grange Farm. Go right of the buildings to a gate and stile ahead, with a drained millpond on the right. While the gate leads to a rough lane, the inviting stile sends a path alongside a drained mill-cut. Emerging into a field, make for a wall-stile in the far corner by some barns.** With a simple weir on Kex Beck, an archway carries wall and path over the cut. **Take the footpath upstream a short way then rise left with the wall to a hidden, crumbling stile, and halt to enjoy the return of the Beacon beyond a gorse bank. Head away with the wall, through another stile to approach Beamsley Hospital. Cross the main road to the almshouses.** Through an arch, a second archway flanked by six almshouses reveals the roundhouse. From a central chapel seven individual rooms radiate, in use until recent times. It is now owned

by the Landmark Trust as a holiday let. A tablet in the main archway
- which originally partnered the Clifford arms above it - is inscribed:

> This almshouse was founded by that excellent lady Margaret
> Russell Countess of Cumberland, wife to George Clifford, third
> Earl of Cumberland 1593, and was more perfectly finished by
> her only child Lady Anne Clifford, now Countess Dowager of
> Pembrooke, Dorsett and Montgomery. God's name be praised.

**Back outside, a path runs up past the postbox to a section of old
road. A rough road goes back sharp left between houses, and leads
unerringly to New Hall Farm. Approaching the farm the path is
diverted right along a wallside, then along from the corner to a
small gate in a fence. Cross to a wall-stile just ahead, then left
across a small enclosure to the lower of two wall-stiles.** Pause for
a prospect ahead of Storiths backed by Earl Seat. Down to the left is
a glimpse of Bolton Priory. **Cross to a wall-stile ahead, then slant up
to the far corner of the field. A stile hidden in the recess sends you
off with the wallside, passing through a stile at the top to find
another onto the lane through Storiths just above. Turn up onto the
back road under colourful Storiths Crag.** Just to the left, Back 'o th'
Hill Farm has a coffee shop with a model railway gallery.

**Turn right, passing Storiths House Farm and taking a stile on the
left before the next farm. Descend to a wall-stile from where a
green way slants up to a fence, then follow it right to a wall-stile.
Now slant across the field to another wall-stile onto a back road
at Hazlewood. Turn left through the hamlet, passing, last of all, the
old school, with its inscribed tablet of 1832. This traffic-free lane
provides a fitting final
promenade over
Beamsley country
before meeting the
old road. The start
is just to the left.**

*The Roundhouse,
Beamsley
Hospital*

## 18

# MIDDLETON MOOR

**START** *Langbar*       *Grid ref. SE 106504*

**DISTANCE** *6 miles (9½ km)*

**ORDNANCE SURVEY MAPS**
*1:50,000*
*Landranger 104 - Leeds, Bradford & Harrogate*
*1:25,000*
*Explorer 297 - Lower Wharfedale & Washburn Valley*

**ACCESS** *Start from the lay-by adjacent to a cattle-grid at Ling Park Plantation, where the road out of Middleton gains the open moor.*

**S** Within the lay-by is an uninspiringly sited Ordnance Survey column at 804ft/245m: it does, however, offer immediate views over Addingham, Chelker windfarm, Barden Moor, Ilkley and Rombalds Moor. **Cross the cattle-grid (1812 boundary stone gatepost) onto Middleton Moor and follow the road outside the plantation, quickly leaving at a bend by a rough road to the right. As the plantation ends remain on the firm track as it runs a splendid course above a wall. At the end it drops slightly to a corner of the moor where the green lanes of Parks Lane and Hunger Hill climb to it.**

An inscribed milestone by the wall has hands pointing the way to Skipton 6m; Ot(t)ley 7m; Rip(p)on 14m; and Ilkley 1m. The latter direction is Parks Lane, the Roman road out of Ilkley. **Ignoring both lanes, turn left with the wall to remain on the moor.** Though the Roman road departs, untracked, off to the right, your way remains a historic route linking Ilkley with the Nidd Valley. **As it forks at the corner, take the left branch directly over the moor,** which these days carries modern transport in the form of shooting parties.

**Whilst apparently heading for complete wilderness, the track runs to meet a wall to shadow it down to a dip, with a wall corner**

**just beyond.** Over it, green fields fall to March Ghyll Reservoir, while up to the left is Beamsley Beacon, from this angle merely a moorland bump. **The shooters' track continues up the wallside, a point to which you shall return. For now, opt for a stile/gate into the grassy pasture alongside. Follow a fence away, briefly, before a stile puts you back onto moorland. A track heads away, crossing Loftshaw Gill, fifty yards beyond which you leave it.**

**Take the gentler left branch up to a shooting butt, bearing right of it and its kin to climb onto the higher tracts of Middleton Moor. It continues ever upwards, through a gate in a fence with a view left to a shooting house in a hollow. In time the wall you left at the bottom returns, parallel with another series of butts.** Looking back there is a fine skyline of Otley Chevin and Rombalds Moor. **Towards the top the way narrows to a slimmer trod, largely a delightful grassy causeway through the heather. Ultimately merging with the wall, the actual bridleway passes through and fades as it crosses to the watershed wall beyond. It is easier however to simply follow the wall along to the wall junction.** The old way continues over the moor to a junction of Kex Gill Road and the modern A59.

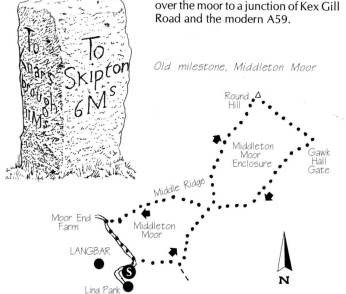

*Old milestone, Middleton Moor*

*Boundary stone on Round Hill*

The panorama opens out, over Beamsley Beacon to Barden Moor. High Dales country is beyond, culminating in Great Whernside's mighty whaleback. Further still are Lancashire's Pendle Hill and Bowland moors. **At the wall junction stands a boundary stone inscribed *MM 1734* in a setting that demands a pause. You are now atop Round Hill, the actual summit marked by a tiny cairn by a big hollow just up behind the wall.** At 1342ft/409m, this is the highest point in the area covered by this guide.

**Depart by turning right (south-east) on a clear path through heather alongside the crumbling wall.** Now there are big views ahead to a sea of moorland, the mast on Norwood Edge, Fewston Reservoir, and Menwith Hill 'golf balls'. **More boundary stones are seen during a pronounced drop,** crossing the indeterminate course of the Roman road. **The wall crumbles into marshy insignificance as your path detours to skirt the moister moments of Thatch Ling, sounding a lot nicer than it looks. The path restores itself on the distinct, heathery Gawk Hall Ridge, quickly reaching an old milestone on a knoll above a substantial wall.** This is a crossroads of ways, your watershed path encountering the historic Ilkley-Ripon track. The milestone's hands point the way to both destinations, that to the north going down through Gawk Hall Gate onto the vastness of Blubberhouses Moor. This is the turning point of the walk.

**Heeding the milestone's advice, turn right with the wall where a broad track takes the Ilkley option. Interestingly, the old road runs a little further from the wall, starting, quite naturally, from the milestone itself. Initially revealing traces of a paved way in the heather, it has largely been reclaimed by the moor. Forging on a little further, however, you might locate a milestone reposed on**

**the ground.** Snapped in two, it still serves its purpose as a hand points forlornly to Ripon. **Beyond it there is no further help, necessitating a skulk back to the rougher track near the wall. This somewhat abused way curves away from the wall as it descends to avoid a marshy area, returning to it in improved fashion to drop through a gate in a fence. Just past it, a thin but clear path branches right, cutting a small corner as it slants down to meet a solid track.** This is the Badger Gate, once patronised by travelling corn dealers, or 'badgers'. **Turn right along this as it runs a level course near the foot of the moor to return to Loftshaw Gill.**

**On re-crossing the stream remain on the track which slants up to a gate in the wall shadowing the shooters' track. Cross straight over, and a greener way heads directly up onto the lower section of Middleton Moor. Soon it gains a brow and runs pleasantly along a modest ridge to a crossroads marked by another old milestone.** This stumpy stone post faithfully records the miles to Skipton (6), Ot(t)ley (5) and Knar(e)sb(o)rough (11), and here the Badger Gate branches right. **Your route simply advances straight on along the brow.** Ahead are Addingham and the Chelker windfarm with a glimpse of the reservoir, with Beamsley Beacon to the right, Rombalds Moor to the left, and the South Craven landmark of Earl Crag and Lancashire's Pendle Hill ahead. **The track soon drops to meet the open road near Moor End Farm. Turn left for a few minutes back to the start, savouring the extensive skyline of Rombalds Moor.**

*Inspecting the milestone at Gawk Hall Gate*

# 19

# KEX GILL MOOR

**START** *Blubberhouses*          *Grid ref.  SE 168553*

**DISTANCE** *5½ miles (9km)*

**ORDNANCE SURVEY MAPS**
*1:50,000*
*Landranger 104 - Leeds, Bradford & Harrogate*
*1:25,000*
*Explorer 297 - Lower Wharfedale & Washburn Valley*

**ACCESS** *Start from Yorkshire Water's Blubberhouses car park on the A59 at the head of Fewston Reservoir. Served by Skipton-Harrogate bus.*

**S** Blubberhouses boasts a name of some jollity, and a reputation for providing the district's first snow-blocked road of the winter. This lonely place is known only for its location astride the busy Skipton to Harrogate road, though the *Hopper Lane* pub up the steep climb towards Harrogate regularly waylays travellers. While this scattered community extends up Hardisty Hill towards Thruscross, St Andrew's church of 1851 sits south of the main road. On a visit in late January its pulpit still wore the decorations of the festive season: the church would have seen its fullest congregations during construction of the reservoirs: Fewston's waters lap right up to the main road.

**Cross the main road and immediately turn off along Hall Lane, rising past Blubberhouses Hall with its mullioned windows. This pleasant climb brings improving views to moorland heights, undeterred by the sound of traffic tearing along the A59. Within a few minutes at a sharp bend, keep straight on up a wide-walled green lane onto Limekiln Hill. This superb track remains the Kex Gill Road throughout its gradual climb, through several pastures before gaining open moorland.** Today it is difficult to imagine it as the only road prior to its parallel southerly replacement. In retrospect the church spire is silhouetted against the waters of Fewston, while

**78**

the great sweep of Blubberhouses Moor fills the scene to the south. Higher up you enter your own heather moor, and can look back to Menwith Hill's 'golf balls'. **At a stile an access track leads up onto a sharp bend of a surfaced road.** To the left of Menwith Hill, the scarp of the Hambleton Hills will be discerned on a clear day.

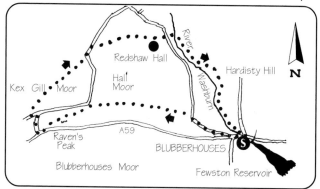

**Continue straight up Kex Gill Road, but leave within 75 yards, turning left before a wall. Quickly bear left from the wall, across open country to reach the edge of a steeper drop towards the main road. A trod runs right to fade just short of a prominent gritstone outcrop on a level with the road-top at Raven's Peak.** Appealing to rock climbers, who know it as Dovestone, it is also a landmark for travellers on the road below. Its flat top makes a splendid place for a break, remembering there is a substantial drop. **From it a clear, thin path contours around to the right, traversing in grand style past a spring.** Note the shoring-up of the road opposite to counteract subsidence: this is the notorious section that winter snowfalls disrupt. **The path runs round above another outcrop to the road summit.**

**Without setting foot on the A59 trace its verge up to a junction, then follow a minor road past an old quarry entrance.** The name Lead Mine Hill confirms this area's mineral extraction credentials. **The road swings right to merge into Kex Gill Road. Go left through the gate and along the abandoned road for 175 yards, to a stile on the right accessing Kex Gill Moor. Doubling back, bear half-right over the moor grass on an inviting little trod. Unfortunately this must soon be abandoned as, merely running parallel with the road, it fails to meet your needs. Instead bear further left over a gentle brow, mingling with heather while earning far-reaching moorland**

**vistas.** Though certainly not evident now, this is the course of an ancient trade route from Ilkley over to the Nidd Valley.

**Gradually descending, aim for a not-too-distant motor road: this tract of moorland is sufficiently small for you to not go drastically wrong.** Dropping to the start of a fence at a line of inferior shooting butts, continue the slant down through denser heather, and a stile will be found in the fence that now doubles back. Below that, two more in succession put you onto that road at Turnwath Bridge.

*At Raven's Peak, Kex Gill*

**Cross the bridge and head up the road - Street Lane - as far as a gate on the right only 50 yards beyond a cattle-grid.** The name 'street' suggests again that this is an old way. **An old green track shadows a wall bending away.** Whilst in its company, note the enticing rock outcrops of Brandrith Crags on Hall Moor to the right. **The track runs a good course through several fields gone to seed (with walls in similar disarray), in time crossing to the wall's other side on the open country of Burnt Hill. At a wall junction further on, ignore the continuing green track, and turn right over a stile into a small field.** Fewston Reservoir returns to the scene straight down the valley.

**Slant down to the bottom corner to enter an abandoned green way down to approach Redshaw Hall.** In the early 1990s a sad case of dereliction, this old farmstead has been impressively restored. **Through a small gate advance along the garden corner to a wall-stile just ahead, from where an enclosed path descends by a tract of new woodland to drop to a stile onto a back road.**

Go left no more than 20 yards to find a quaint little flight of steps descending from the wall on the right. **A good little path slants down to a stile into a plantation, then down onto the access road to Thruscross Reservoir. Go right a few strides and then double back left onto a track just below. This too is quickly abandoned in favour of a more inviting path doubling back to the right.** Back up to the left is the massive concrete dam, 600ft long and 120ft high. This is by far the youngest of the Washburn lakes, constructed as recently as 1966. Sacrificed was the hamlet of West End, which has since returned to daylight in times of drought. **The path runs into trees and quickly along to a ford and footbridge on the River Washburn. Turn downstream in lovely surrounds.**

**Within a couple of minutes a boulder-strewn plantation comes in to the bank, and the path forks.** The public footpath bears left along its base with a drained water cut. A track comes up to bridge the cut, up through trees and along to Scaife Hall Farm, then out along its drive and up to the Greenhow Hill road. **Best option is the water company's permissive path that remains with the river, which provides delectable company. The way includes a spell alongside a pleasant dam before the river leads on past the idyllically sited cricket club to reach steps up onto the A59 opposite the car park.**

St. Andrew's, Blubberhouses

## 20

# BLUBBERHOUSES MOOR

**START** *Timble    Grid ref. SE 179529*

**DISTANCE** *6½ miles (10½km)*

**ORDNANCE SURVEY MAPS**
*1:50,000*
*Landranger 104 - Leeds, Bradford & Harrogate*
*1:25,000*
*Explorer 297 - Lower Wharfedale & Washburn Valley*

**ACCESS** *Start from the village centre: considerate roadside parking.*

**S** Little more than a hamlet, Timble has long been a favourite with local walkers. The Timble Inn re-opened in 2009 after several years closed. The settlement sits astride a modest ridge which becomes immediately evident on beginning the walk. Across the street is the Institute (Robinson Gill Library and Free School), which has its own story at the start of WALK 21. **Leave the village by the road rising out past the millennium oak.** At once wide views are the order of the day as you march along a distinct ridge: great sweeps of moorland are dissected by the hand of man, with the 'golf balls' at Menwith Hill base, Norwood Edge and its mast, and Thruscross's dam slotting into place over to the right. **Keep straight on past the Fewston junction to a crossroads at Timble Lane End.**

**Cross this potentially dangerous brow with care, and a rough road heads past the few dwellings at Sourby towards a plantation. At a junction just past a covered reservoir, the main way goes on into the trees, while the walk opts for a solid track branching left. At a cattle-grid it gains the open moor, marching up the heather past several boundary stones.** Look back to savour a particularly colourful prospect of the shapely Washburn Valley. **The track rises to a sharply-angled wall-corner on Ellarcarr Pike, where it swings right to serve Eller Carr Farm.**

This grassy knoll is a super spot supporting a pair of boundary stones, one dated 1825. Ahead are views over the impending moors and across Wharfedale to a Rombalds Moor skyline, while nearer to hand is the greenery of the plantation: a clear day reveals the White Horse of Kilburn beyond Menwith Hill. **A path for Denton heads directly away, while yours is that going right with the wall. Cross the stile and head off on the heather path known as High Badger Gate ('badger' being the old name for a corn dealer), across the upper reaches of Denton Moor: several moist sections are encountered. With a plantation over the wall on the right, the path approaches the heathery spur of Lippersley Ridge.**

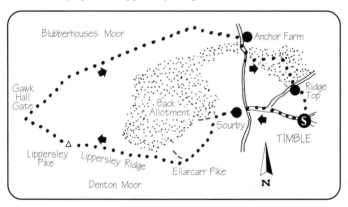

At a junction a branch runs right to the plantation corner, while your way mounts the ridge to a prominent boundary stone. Here another path linking with the previous branch comes in. Re-united, the way rises to a big cairn on Lippersley Pike. This proves to be hollow, yet is not a shelter as there is no entrance. The OS map denotes it as a cairn of antiquity: whatever, it is certainly a grand place to be, afloat in a sea of wild moorland. Alongside is a boundary stone inscribed 1767.

**Resume along the obvious continuation path which makes for Gawk Hill Ridge under the skyline ahead. Head half-right off the knoll, descending quite steeply to cross the neck of marshy Stainforth Gill Head. After a few moist moments the path makes for another heathery knoll, climbing to run along the increasingly lovely but short-lived edge of Gawk Hill Ridge. The sturdy wall beyond is the turning point of the walk. Cross the stile and inspect**

**the old milestone (see page 77).** It is inscribed with hands pointing the way, and distances, to Ilkley and Rip(p)on, and serves to indicate that this was an important trading route between these market towns.

*On Lippersley Pike*

**Leave by turning right on the track (the old moorland road itself) to cross a tiny stream to Gawk Hall Gate. Sloping up the low bank behind, the track bears right to begin a long, steady slant away from the wall and marshy stream. Some early sections, once a quagmire, are less tortuous since vehicular use has been banned: nevertheless some unsavoury moments remain! Heading directly for the 'golf balls' at Menwith Hill, there seems little promise of improvement as Blubberhouses Moor stretches endlessly away, but things soon pick up.** Over to the right is a large plantation, while there is a glimpse of Fewston Reservoir ahead. **Conditions improve at a major turning point as the track swings right, picking up a slim trod that marks the course of the Roman road.** Thought to date from the 1st century, it traverses the Pennines from Manchester to Aldborough, near Boroughbridge, via of course, Ilkley.

**Allied to a reedy drain known as the Runner, this track continues its gentle descent of the moor as a distinct causeway in comparatively excellent condition.** At once, observe that lifting your eyes along the track, the main A59 road is precisely in line, confirming its Roman origins. **The track descends unfailingly to ford Sun Bank Gill, with a vast plantation well over to the right across the valley. Rising up the other side a long, level section ensues, now a superb grassy way: still the Roman A59 guides. As a gradual descent**

returns, another green track comes in on the left, but quickly bears off right leaving you to continue down to a marshy saddle. The track heads up the bracken slopes of tiny Cote Hill, then along its brow before finally losing the line of the Romans (which in any case descends the fields to be drowned in Fewston's waters).

While the track bears down to the left and the invisible Roman way marches straight on, the walk takes neither. At the demise of the bracken on your right, turn sharp right and cross to the nearby wall, with the foot of Fewston Reservoir as a guide. Bear right with it to quickly reach a gate at a slight kink in it. Leaving the moor follow the wallside down the field, descending a second field then crossing to a gate in the far corner above a plantation. Here you join the Blubberhouses-Otley road opposite Anchor Farm.

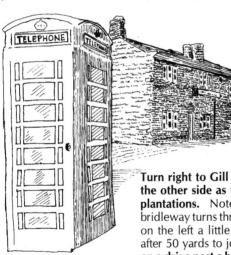

*At Timble: traditional inn and traditional phone box*

**Turn right to Gill Beck Bridge, and up the other side as far as the end of the plantations.** Note that a permissive bridleway turns through a gate into trees on the left a little earlier, turning right after 50 yards to join the drive. **Go left on a drive past a barn to enter Beecroft Moor Plantation.** After a few minutes look out for a signed footpath crossing the forest road. Turn up an initially unconvincing path to the right, which provides a pleasant climb through native woodland and dense bilberry to a stile onto a road opposite Ridge Top Farm. Cross to a stile in front and slant left to a stile in the wall across the field. Rise to a gateway on a brow with the houses of Timble in front, and advance through crumbling gateways and walls to pass left of the nearest house and up onto the road through the village.

# 21

# SWINSTY & FEWSTON

**START** Timble        Grid ref. SE 179529

**DISTANCE** 6 miles (9½km)

## ORDNANCE SURVEY MAPS
1:50,000
Landranger 104 - Leeds, Bradford & Harrogate
1:25,000
Explorer 297 - Lower Wharfedale & Washburn Valley

**ACCESS** Start from the village centre, roadside parking. Alternative
start points are Yorkshire Water car parks at Stack Point (GR 198537)
and Swinsty Moor (GR 186537). The walk passes through both.

**S** Timble is a peaceful village on a broad ridge descending from
the moors to the Washburn Valley. The Timble Inn re-opened in a
new style in 2009 after several years closed. Across the street is the
Robinson Gill Library and Free School, the gift in 1891 of a local lad
who found fortune in America. The stonemason who built it was John
Dickinson, another local worthy greatly influenced by Gill's achieve-
ments. His own modest yet absorbing life story has been brought to
light after discovery of diaries of his last 34 years resulted in the book
*Timble Man - Diaries of a Dalesman.*

**Facing the *Timble Inn* alongside the phone box, take the byway to
its left to join and go left along a back road.** Enjoy immediately
glorious views down the Washburn Valley. **As it leaves the houses,
look for a delightful walled path branching left. On expiring in a
field advance to a gate ahead, where the Menwith Hill 'golf balls'
make an eerie appearance. Bear left to a line of trees and descend
the fieldsides. Approaching a plantation bear slightly right down
to a gate into the trees. A broad path descends to a wall-stile into the
grounds of Swinsty Hall.** Just before this point a permissive path slants
left, but this bizarre option would omit the delights of the old house.

**Drop left on the drive towards the hall.** Swinsty Hall is a stunning discovery in the middle of nowhere: at one time it would have looked across a green valley floor to the village of Fewston, a very different scene! Built in 1570, its first occupants forfeited it to a moneylender whose family kept hold for 300 years. Until 1992 it spent a quarter-century in the hands of a distinguished Yorkshire musician, who played concerts in its atmospheric surroundings. The irregular gabled facade with its three storeyed porch makes a fine scene, ably supported by a criss-cross of mullioned and transomed windows.

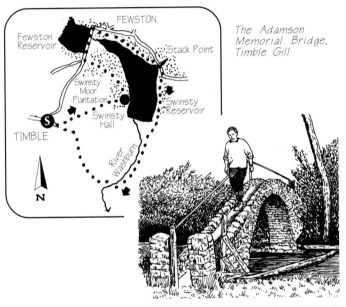

*The Adamson Memorial Bridge, Timble Gill*

**Pass left of the hall to a wall-stile hidden to the left of the gate. Back in the trees, don't descend the track but rise a few feet to advance along a broad track through the plantations.** With occasional glimpses into Swinsty Reservoir it runs to Swinsty Moor car park, with WC and fishing office. **Turn down the road to cross Fewston embankment.** Enjoying views over both reservoirs constructed in the 1870s, each covers 153 acres and holds 850 million gallons. **Immediately across turn down to the right, where steps drop onto a zealously manufactured path along Swinsty's eastern shore, an enjoyable walk that curves around to Stack Point car park.**

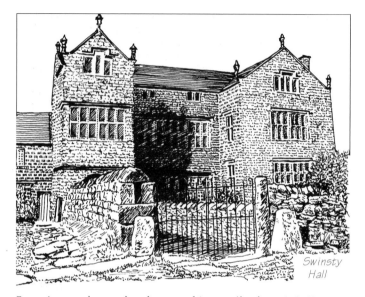

*Swinsty Hall*

Emerging on the road, a feature of interest back up it is Fewston church. This could be reached more directly by staying on the road at the end of Fewston embankment, but at the expense of the Swinsty shore walk to Stack Point. It is difficult now to imagine Fewston as the active community it was before the reservoirs came. Graced with a wonderful setting, St Lawrence's church boasts a solid 14th century tower. The rest was rebuilt in 1697 after a fire, making it a rare and outstanding example of church architecture of that period: observe the original thatched roof-line of the old nave on the tower wall. Amongst the absorbing gravestones the best known bears a date 30th February. Between Fewston House and the church is a purpose-built viewpoint, with wooden seats overlooking a break in the trees to savour a big Washburn scene over Swinsty Reservoir.

**Back at Stack Point, advance along the embankment with the attractive Swinsty Lagoon on the left. Immediately across, take a gate on the right and resume the shore walk, an artificial path running between Swinsty Woods and the shore. Reaching a water company road, turn right on it to the keeper's house.** Passed en route is an ornate 'shed' hiding a brass plaque recording the opening of the reservoir by Leeds Corporation Waterworks.

This time shunning the embankment, take a gate on the left and head away towards a pine plantation on the left. A grassy terrace precedes a pleasant drop towards the riverbank. A stile in a wall at the bottom sees a thin path head off downstream. Lined by trees the river makes a good companion, when it is allowed to flow. The surroundings remain entirely delightful, with a glimpse of moorland above a steep wooded bank. **The way runs pleasantly along to a bridge below the wooded spur of Sword Point. Cross it and resume downstream to quickly arrive at inflowing Timble Gill Beck.** This may well have more life than the Washburn itself. Though not crossed, it should be inspected to see the charming Adamson Memorial Bridge, a miniature packhorse bridge erected in 1966 in memory of a Leeds alderman who campaigned for walkers' rights.

**Turning up by the gill, a crumbling wall comes in before you rise to a gateway to be deflected above the steep wooded bank. Climbing outside the trees, when it drops away retain the delight-ful bank top to a stile in a tiny section of wall at the end, and along a fenceside to a gate.** The deep bowl of the gill below was the haunt of the Timble Witches, less infamous than their Pendle sisters, but enough of a threat to have faced assizes at York. **Don't pass through but turn up the near side of the rebuilt wall. From the top corner stile, cross a small corner of tree plantings to another stile then resume up a wallside as Timble re-appears. A stile at the top admits onto a rough lane.**
**Turn left to absorb the outward route.**

*The Institute (Robinson Gill Library and Free School). Timble*

# 22

# LINDLEY WOOD

**START** Leathley          Grid ref. SE 232470

**DISTANCE** 7½ miles (12km)

**ORDNANCE SURVEY MAPS**
1:50,000
Landranger 104 - Leeds, Bradford & Harrogate
1:25,000
Explorer 297 - Lower Wharfedale & Washburn Valley

**ACCESS** Start from the roadside brow opposite the church on the
B6161. There is a small parking area here.

**S** The scattered community of Leathley is centred on St Oswald's
church, sat proudly on a knoll embowered in Scots Pine. It boasts a
magnificent Norman tower and a nave from the same period, in the
west doorway of which a Norman door is richly decorated with
ironwork. The woodcraft of the Thompson workshops of Kilburn is
evidenced by the mouse symbol on many items of furniture. Also on
this brow are the picturesque almshouses and old school, founded in
1769. Their endowment is recorded on a tablet by the entrance.

**Turning north along the roadside footway, a milestone opposite
informs you this is the Dudley Hill, Killinghall and Harrogate road.
From a stile on the left just past it and a side junction, cross the field
to a wooden footbridge slung over the River Washburn. Turning
right up the side of this extensive crop field, a path briefly shadows
the river. Soon woodland intervenes, whence continue up the field
outside a plantation. Your way rises in splendid fashion to the field
top to meet a road.**

**Turning right, a verge of sorts provides some assistance.** Woodland opposite marks the immediate grounds of the real hall, which
might be glimpsed through the slender trunks. Farnley Hall is a part
Elizabethan house, added to by the architect John Carr in the late

1780s. It was the seat of the Fawkes family for centuries, and known for its large collection of Turners. Walter Fawkes was a patron of the artist, who himself was a frequent visitor here - as was the Victorian writer, artist and conservationist John Ruskin.

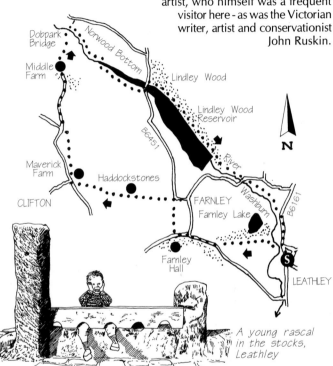

A young rascal in the stocks, Leathley

**At Home Farm, with its traditional courtyard, a junction is reached alongside a lodge. The B6451 goes right while the hall drive goes left: note a memorial tap. A few minutes further, with a proper footway now, a stile opposite gives access to park-like grounds. Follow the hedgerow away, undulating towards Farnley church.** Surviving kerbstones confirm this as an old way from hall to church. **At the end slant right up to a stile into the church car park.** The modest little All Saints church was rebuilt in 1851. **Joining the road, go left a few yards past a cottage and onto Haddockstones farm drive.** This offers views over to Otley Chevin and the more laid-back Rombalds Moor. **This solid way is traced until a sharp turn for the farm, whereupon keep straight on a part-kerbed way by the fence.**

Over to the right is the bank of Haddockstones Plantation, which has grown around a group of old delphs. The stone quarried here was a gift from the Farnley Hall estate for the building of Newall workhouse at Otley, later part of the Wharfedale General Hospital. Looking back, mile upon mile of the Wharfe Valley is now on parade, down to Arthington Viaduct on the Leeds-Harrogate line. **As the track enters the top end of the wood keep outside the wall enclosing it, maintaining this line along an extended, well-defined bank top as a TV mast appears ahead. Ignore a stile above a sunken green way dropping to a farm, instead finding your stile in a wall at the very end. Cross a tiny beck and the brow behind to locate a stile onto the Otley-Blubberhouses road at a junction.**

**A green verge leads right a short way, passing the mast's access road and Maverick Farm drive. Immediately after, use a stile in the wall to run parallel through the field to a stile level with the farm buildings. Advance on keeping left of all buildings, as a track heads away through a couple more stiles before petering out. Simply advance on through a gate/stile in a wall, and cross one further field to a stile in the wall corner ahead. Here the traffic-free, cul-de-sac road to Dob Park is joined, descending between wide verges with excellent views over the Washburn Valley.**

**Further down the road winds down a steep wooded bank prior to its demise at Middle Farm. A rough lane takes over to snake along the valley floor. The lane runs on to arrive at the celebrated Dobpark Bridge.** This fine old bridge gracefully arches the wooded Washburn, matched by setts running down to a ford: it is the unofficial emblem of Washburn country.

*Dobpark Bridge*

Leave the old road climbing the bank, and opt for a stile on the right from where a path runs downstream through leafy Norwood Bottom, quickly joining a broader pathway. While not in intimate contact with the river, it does afford good views over it to a wider landscape. After crossing an open pasture the way is taken across the river's tree-lined course on a water company bridge. The path resumes downstream towards the reedy head of Lindley Wood Reservoir, winding through verdant surrounds to meet a road.

Cross the viaduct and turn right through a gateway on the opposite bank, where a carriageway plunges into the trees. The track runs close to the edge of the 117-acre reservoir constructed by Leeds Corporation in 1875. The entire way remains unexpectedly non-claustrophobic to reach the large dam alongside its vast concrete outflow. The track forges on to return to the trees, rising and running along to emerge alongside a lodge on a winding road. Turn down to look over Lindley Bridge, then take a gap on your side to descend a flight of stone steps.

A path squeezes between mill goit and fish hatchery, one restored to supply the other. Past them the drained channel is followed for some time before dropping down to the river to head downstream on a potentially moist section of path. Things pick up quickly and the cut returns as company to Mill House, the former Leathley Mill. Turn up its near side to emerge onto a road. The church is a short half-mile to the right, passing Leathley's exclusive properties as the verge-cum-footway leads back to the start.

St Oswald's,
Leathley

# LOG OF THE WALKS

| WALK | DATE | NOTES |
|------|------|-------|
| 1 | | |
| 2 | | |
| 3 | | |
| 4 | | |
| 5 | | |
| 6 | | |
| 7 | | |
| 8 | | |
| 9 | | |
| 10 | | |
| 11 | | |
| 12 | | |
| 13 | | |
| 14 | | |
| 15 | | |
| 16 | | |
| 17 | | |
| 18 | | |
| 19 | | |
| 20 | | |
| 21 | | |
| 22 | | |

# SOME USEFUL ADDRESSES

**Ramblers' Association**
2nd Floor, Camelford House, 87-89 Albert Embankment, London SE1 7BR
Tel. 020-7339 8500

*Tourist Information*

Station Road **Ilkley**  Tel. 01943-602319

35 Coach Street **Skipton** Tel. 01756-792809

Otley Library, Nelson Street **Otley** Tel. 01943-466572

Royal Baths Assembly Rooms, Crescent Road **Harrogate**
Tel. 01423-537300

**Yorkshire Dales National Park**
Colvend, Hebden Road, Grassington, Skipton BD23 5LB
Tel. 01756-751600

**Yorkshire Dales Society**
Town Hall, Cheapside, Settle BD24 9EJ
Tel. 01729-825600

**Public transport**
Traveline
0870-608 2608

**National Rail
Enquiry Line**
08457-484950

*Main entrance,
Beamsley Hospital*

# INDEX

## *Principal features (walk number refers)*

| | | | |
|---|---|---|---|
| Addingham | 11,12,13 | Hazlewood | 17 |
| | | Heber's Ghyll | 13 |
| Baildon | 4 | Holden Beck | 7 |
| Baildon Moor | 4 | Horncliffe | 2 |
| Barden Moor | 10 | | |
| Beamsley | 17 | Ilkley | 3,13,14,15,16 |
| Beamsley Beacon | 17 | Ilkley Crags | 15 |
| Bingley Moor | 6 | Ilkley Moor | 3,14,15 |
| Blubberhouses | 19 | | |
| Blubberhouses Moor | 20 | Kex Gill Moor | 19 |
| Bolton Abbey | 10 | Kildwick | 8 |
| Bolton Bridge | 10 | | |
| Bradley | 9 | Langbar | 17,18 |
| Buck Stones | 14 | Leathley | 22 |
| Burley Moor | 2,3,6,15 | Leeds-Liverpool Canal | 5,6,8,9 |
| Burley Woodhead | 2,3 | Lindley Wood Reservoir | 22 |
| | | Lippersley Pike | 20 |
| Caley Crags | 1 | | |
| Chelker Reservoir | 12 | Menston | 3 |
| Cow & Calf Rocks | 3 | Micklethwaite | 6 |
| Cowper's Cross | 14 | Middleton | 16 |
| Crossflatts | 6 | Middleton Moor | 18 |
| | | Middleton Woods | 16 |
| Danefield | 1 | Myddelton Lodge | 16 |
| Denton | 16 | | |
| Dick Hudson's | 5,15 | Otley Chevin | 1 |
| Doubler Stones | 7 | | |
| Draughton | 10,11 | Raven's Peak | 19 |
| | | Round Hill | 18 |
| East Morton | 6 | | |
| | | Saltaire | 5 |
| Farnhill | 8 | Shipley Glen | 5 |
| Farnhill Moor | 8 | Skipton | 11 |
| Farnley | 22 | Skipton Moor | 9 |
| Faweather Grange | 2,4 | Snaygill | 9 |
| Fewston | 21 | Storiths | 17 |
| Fewston Reservoir | 20,21 | Sunnydale | 6 |
| Five Rise Locks | 6 | Swastika Stone | 3,14 |
| | | Swinsty | 21 |
| Grubstones | 2 | | |
| | | Thimble Stones | 6 |
| Halton East | 10 | Timble | 20,21 |
| Hawksworth | 4 | Twelve Apostles | 15 |
| Hawksworth Moor | 2 | | |
| | | Washburn, river | 19,21,22 |
| | | Wharfe, river | 3,12,13,16 |